Cover Photo: Bean Spread with Nachips, Chicken Tacos (bowls/
taco sauce/lettuce/onions/tomatoes), Hearty Beefy Enchiladas,
Mexican Corn Bread.

Preceding page: Chilies Rellenos

SUN COUNTRY MEXICAN COOKBOOK II

Produced by

PET

An **IC Industries** Company

Grocery Products Division

Pet Incorporated
St. Louis, MO 63166

Recipes developed and tested
by Home Economists in Pet Kitchens.

OLD EL PASO Nachips

...HIPS FOR NACHOS,
...AND SNACKS

OLD EL PASO 12 Tostada Shells

NET WT. 5 OZ. 141g

OLD EL PASO 12 Taco Sh...

NET WT. 4½ OZ. 127g

SHAKE WELL

OLD EL PASO MILD Taco Sauce 16 OZ

OLD EL PASO HOT Taco Sauce 16 OZ

OLD EL PASO Retried Beans with Sausage

OLD EL PASO Retried Beans

OLD EL PASO Pickled Hot Jalapeño Strips FOR NACHOS AND PIZZA

OLD EL PASO Pickled Chilies Jalapeños

SHAKE WELL

TABLE OF CONTENTS

Dinner (Overleaf): Tomato Chili Cheese Soup, Chicken Chilies Rellenos, Mexican Rice, Four-Bean Salad, Toasted Bananas.

Culture and History of Mexican Food

Mexican cuisine has its origin around 5,000 B.C. with the first cultivation of corn. Through the succeeding 6,500 years, a succession of Mexican Indian cultures expanded and enhanced this cuisine. The last of the great Indian cultures was the Aztec. This highly sophisticated society built beautiful temples and developed a calendar system which, in the 15th century, was more accurate than that used in Europe. Then, in the early 16th century, the Spaniards conquered Mexico, destroying most of the native civilization.

The Spanish came in search of gold and silver; but as they conquered the land, they also settled, and soon monks and nuns were coming to the new country. The Spanish nuns were the first to combine the native agricultural foods of the Aztecs with the onions, garlic, rice, nuts and olive oil brought from Spain. Many of their creations have become Mexico's favorite dishes.

Today, the cuisine of Mexico is a rich blend of Indian and Spanish with French and Italian influences. Much of the food is earthy, developed by peasants with ingredients on hand. Some is also elegant. But it is always colorful, full of texture contrasts and uniquely Mexican.

Corn, beans, chilies and tomatoes grown by the early Aztecs are still the staples in the Mexican kitchen. Corn is the country's major crop. When ground into "masa," it is used for making tortillas, the "bread" of Mexico.

Tortillas play a key role in the Mexican menu, not only as the "staff of life" but in other foods as well. Tortillas are never wasted. They are folded, fried and filled to make "tacos." They are toasted flat and topped with beans, meat and a sauce for "tostadas." They are rolled around meat or cheese and baked with a sauce for "enchiladas." They are folded around fillings for "burritos." And when they are stale, they are cut into pieces for casseroles or fried crisp for soups.

Mexico's best known ingredient—and the one that gives the food its characteristic flavor—is the chili. Chilies of many varieties are used in the Mexican kitchen ranging from sweet to fiery hot. Chilies and tomatoes, seasoned with onions and herbs, are the basis for the many sauces that are as common on the table as "salt and pepper." A more complicated chili sauce, called mole, is used in meat dishes.

In addition to the traditional ingredients, an abundance of fruits and vegetables are grown in Mexico. The most widely used is the avocado, often for guacamole. Citrus fruits, tropical fruits and parts of the cactus are also plentiful. Beef, pork and chicken are Mexico's basic meats although fish and seafood are widely used, particularly in Mexico's coastal regions.

Climate and geography in Mexico have a much greater effect on the cuisine than in the United States. High, rugged mountains separate many regions of Mexico into local entities. For many years this led to very distinct regional cooking which, to a great extent, continues today. Each region has its own food specialties, some based on produce and meats of the area, others on unwritten recipes passed down from generation to generation.

In this country Mexican food has been widely used for years in the Southwest. In fact, it is so much a part of the Southwestern menu that an adapted version is called "Tex-Mex." Tex-Mex favorites, tacos, tostadas, enchiladas, burritos and guacamole, are often "hotter and spicier" than their Mexican originals.

In the last few years, travel and Mexican restaurants have introduced all Americans to the tastes and pleasures of Mexican food. People everywhere have discovered that Mexican food is delicious, nutritious and not expensive.

Traditional Mexican dishes often take many hours of cooking. Chilies must be roasted and peeled; tortillas, shaped and fried; and beans and sauces simmered for hours. Old El Paso has eliminated this work in its line of Mexican products. With Old El Paso chilies, tortillas, taco shells, refried beans, sauces and other products anyone can "cook Mexican" at home.

This all-new Sun Country cookbook offers many exciting new Mexican recipes. Some are Tex-Mex, some are native Mexican dishes. All can be made in any American kitchen.

Lunch (Overleaf): Mexican Stuffed Zucchini, Quesadillas (garnished with guacamole/sour cream), Relishes—garbanzos, chopped chilies, piquant sauce.

HINTS FOR COOKING MEXICAN FOODS

1. When frying tortillas, make sure oil is near 375°F, or that tortilla sizzles when it touches hot fat. Use only a deep fry/fat thermometer.

2. To fry tortillas until limp, hold with tongs and quickly dip in hot oil on each side to get proper texture. Drain on paper towels.

3. To fry tortillas until crisp, place in hot oil for 8 to 10 seconds until light brown and slightly puffed. Drain on paper towels.

4. To heat flour tortillas in the microwave oven, wrap tortillas in a moist towel. Microcook for 1 to 2 minutes or until soft and warm.

5. Oil that has been used for frying can be used over again, provided it is strained and refrigerated after use.

6. If not frying tortillas and you want to get them flexible enough to work with, brush with oil, wrap in foil and steam in 350°F oven for 5 minutes.

7. If you plan to let tortillas sit out awhile, be sure to wrap them airtight in foil or plastic wrap to prevent drying. If edges should get dry, brush with oil or butter.

8. Before making dishes that call for fried tortillas, remember to have all fillings and garnishes ready. Work fast so the tortillas don't dry out.

9. When making tortilla dishes that call for fried corn or flour tortillas to be filled, go through the whole process one at a time. If all tortillas are fried at first, they will get tough or stiff and may tear when trying to roll.

10. The word "taco" means a "snack." Quesadillas and chimichangas are merely varieties of a taco.

11. Tostadas are also a "finger food." No use trying to take a fork and knife to one.

12. The preferred Mexican way to use meat is to shred it for tacos, enchiladas, casseroles, etc. You may want to substitute shredded leftover meat, e.g. chicken, beef, instead of the ground beef called for in some recipes.

13. The use of chilies typifies Mexican cooking. Not all are hot and fiery. Many are mild and richly flavored. For a hotter Tex-Mex Mexican flavor, use Old El Paso Jalapenos in place of Old El Paso Green Chilies in recipes. Jalapenos add a high heat level so use with caution.

14. Old El Paso Taco Sauce is available in hot and mild varieties. The hot variety has chopped jalapenos as an ingredient for the greater heat level. The mild variety uses green chilies for a pleasingly mild taco sauce. The same is true with mild and hot enchilada sauces.

15. Refried beans can be served anytime of day, with a hearty mid-morning breakfast, with a midday meal or for supper. Refried beans are an excellent source of protein and are also very economically priced. For variety try refried beans with green chilies or sausage in any recipe calling for refried beans or serve plain, warmed, as a dip or side dish. These varieties are particularly good as a filling for tacos and tostadas.

16. If you are just beginning to start Mexican cooking, there is no need to plan and prepare a whole fiesta. Try one dish at a time. Mexican dishes complement any meal.

17. There are two general methods for making rolled enchiladas: (1) tortillas are softened in hot fat, dipped into a sauce, filled and rolled, (2) or simply dipped into hot fat, filled, rolled and the sauce poured over the top—as we have indicated throughout this cookbook.

18. Enchiladas may also be made with the tortillas stacked with filling in between, baked and cut into pie-shaped wedges.

19. Many Mexican dishes may be cooked in the microwave oven. Microwave instructions have been included for recipes in this book. Because of different wattages, cooking time in your oven may differ. For best results, consult your microwave oven manufacturer's guide. Be sure to use microwave proof dishes, of course!

APPETIZERS

Delicious, and with jalapenos, a bit hot!

JALAPENO BEAN DIP

1 can (16 oz.) OLD EL PASO Refried Beans or OLD EL PASO
Refried Beans with Green Chilies or OLD EL PASO
Refried Beans with Sausage

1 can (7½ oz.) OLD EL PASO Jalapeno Relish

½ cup (2 oz.) shredded Cheddar cheese

¼ teaspoon onion salt

OLD EL PASO NACHIPS Tortilla Chips

Combine beans, jalapeno relish, cheese and onion salt in
saucepan. Cook over medium heat until steaming. Serve warm or
cold with NACHIPS.

MICROCOOK uncovered on 70% power for 6 to 8 minutes or until
heated through.

JALAPENO CHEESE BALL

5 OLD EL PASO Jalapeno Peppers

1 pound shredded sharp Cheddar cheese

1 large onion, quartered

3 cloves garlic, minced

½ cup mayonnaise

1 cup chopped pecans

OLD EL PASO NACHIPS Tortilla Chips

Remove tops and seeds from peppers. Combine peppers, cheese,
onion and garlic. Grate finely with food processor, food grater or
grinder. Mix in mayonnaise. Chill until firm; form into ball. Roll in
pecans. Serve with NACHIPS. Makes 1 large ball.

Preceding page: Cheesy Shrimp Dip, Guacamole, Jalapeno Cheese Ball

PIMIENTO CHEESE DIP

2 cups (8 oz.) shredded process pimiento cheese

½ cup sour cream

1 package (3 oz.) cream cheese, softened

½ cup OLD EL PASO Taco Sauce

1 can (4 oz.) OLD EL PASO Chopped Green Chilies

4 slices bacon, crisp-cooked, drained and crumbled

⅛ teaspoon cayenne pepper

OLD EL PASO NACHIPS Tortilla Chips

In small mixing bowl, combine pimiento cheese, sour cream, cream cheese, taco sauce and green chilies. Beat until light and fluffy. Stir in crumbled bacon and pepper. Chill. Serve with vegetable dippers and/or NACHIPS.

TACO CHICKEN WINGS

2½ pounds chicken wings

2 cups dry bread crumbs

1 envelope (1¼ oz.) OLD EL PASO Taco Seasoning Mix

1 jar (16 oz.) OLD EL PASO Taco Sauce

Remove wing tips and discard. Cut wings at joint. Combine bread crumbs and taco seasoning mix; mix well. Preheat oven to 375°F. Dip each chicken piece in taco sauce; roll in bread crumbs; coat thoroughly. Place on a lightly greased baking sheet. Bake for 30 to 35 minutes.

TEXAS STYLE NACHOS

1 cup (8 oz.) pasteurized process cheese spread

1 box (7½ oz.) OLD EL PASO NACHIPS Tortilla Chips

1 can (4 oz.) OLD EL PASO Chopped Green Chilies, drained

OLD EL PASO Taco Sauce

sour cream

guacamole (see recipe page 19)

Heat process cheese spread. On serving dish, layer half of the tortilla chips, green chilies and process cheese spread. Repeat layers. Top with taco sauce, if desired. Serve with sour cream and guacamole.

MICROCOOK cheese spread in a small bowl on 50% power for 4 minutes or until melted. Stir after two minutes.

BEEF AND BEAN EMPANADAS

5 PET-RITZ "Deep Dish" Pie Crust Shells

½ pound ground beef

1 medium onion, chopped

½ cup OLD EL PASO Mild Taco Sauce or Tomatoes and Jalapeno Peppers

1 cup OLD EL PASO Refried Beans or OLD EL PASO Refried Beans with Green Chilies or OLD EL PASO Refried Beans with Sausage

½ teaspoon salt

¼ teaspoon pepper

PET Evaporated Milk

OLD EL PASO Taco Sauce

Remove pie crusts from freezer. Invert onto waxed paper. Let thaw until flat. Meanwhile, brown ground beef and onion in large skillet. Drain fat. Add taco sauce, beans, salt and pepper. Heat; set aside, cool to room temperature. Role each pie crust on a lightly floured surface to a 12-inch circle. Cut each crust into 10 2½-inch circles with a biscuit cutter. Preheat oven to 400°F. Spoon 1 teaspoon of the cooled filling onto one side of pastry circle. Fold pastry over filling. Seal edges with tines of fork. Place on a well-greased baking sheet. Brush with evaporated milk. Bake until lightly browned, about 15 to 20 minutes. Serve with taco sauce. Makes 50 empanadas.

NOTE: Reroll scraps of pie crust dough to make additional empanadas. Empanadas can be made ahead and frozen. Reheat before serving.

GUACAMOLE

2 large ripe avocados, peeled, pitted and sliced

1 jar (8 oz.) OLD EL PASO Taco Sauce

½ cup chopped onion

2 tablespoons lemon or lime juice

1 teaspoon salt

½ teaspoon garlic powder

1 box (7½ oz.) OLD EL PASO NACHIPS Tortilla Chips

Blend avocado slices, taco sauce, onion, juice, salt and garlic powder in blender or food processor. Chill. Serve with NACHIPS.

Appetizers (Overleaf): Beef and Bean Empanadas, Chili Con Queso/Nachip Dip, Enchilada Meatballs, Taco Chicken Wings, Nachos.

BEAN SPREAD

1 can (16 oz.) OLD EL PASO Refried Beans or OLD EL PASO
   Refried Beans with Green Chilies or OLD EL PASO
   Refried Beans with Sausage

1 tablespoon Worcestershire sauce

½ teaspoon garlic salt

3 drops liquid hot pepper sauce

¼ cup (1 oz.) shredded Cheddar cheese

1 box (7½ oz.) OLD EL PASO NACHIPS Tortilla Chips

Combine beans, Worcestershire sauce, garlic salt and liquid hot
pepper sauce in a small saucepan. Heat to steaming. Spoon into
serving dish and top with shredded cheese. Garnish as desired.
Serve as a spread or dip for NACHIPS. Makes 2 cups.

NOTE: For a spicier spread use 1 can (10½ oz.) OLD EL PASO
   Jalapeno Bean Dip in place of beans.

CHILI CHEESE CRISP

2 flour tortillas, 10 or 12-inch

1 tablespoon butter, softened

1 cup (4 oz.) shredded Monterey Jack cheese

1 cup (4 oz.) shredded Cheddar cheese

1 can (4 oz.) OLD EL PASO Chopped Green Chilies
   OLD EL PASO Taco Sauce

Preheat oven to broil. Brush tortillas with butter and place on a
well-greased baking sheet. Brown lightly under broiler. Remove
and top with cheeses and green chilies. Broil to melt cheese. To
serve, tear apart or cut in wedges with scissors or sharp knife. Top
with taco sauce before serving. Makes 6 servings.

Variations: If desired, top with sliced olives and mushrooms before
   baking, or after baking, top with shredded lettuce and
   diced tomatoes, then taco sauce.

CHILI CON QUESO/NACHIP DIP

1 can (10 oz.) OLD EL PASO Tomatoes and Green Chilies

4 cups (1 lb.) shredded American cheese

1 box (7½ oz.) OLD EL PASO NACHIPS Tortilla Chips

Combine tomatoes and green chilies and cheese in small
saucepan. Cook over medium heat until cheese is smooth and
melted. Serve warm with NACHIPS. Makes about 2¼ cups.

MICROCOOK uncovered on 50% power for 8 to 10 minutes or
until heated through. Stir every two minutes.

CHEESE CHILI PIZZA

1 pound ground beef

1 envelope (1¼ oz.) OLD EL PASO Taco Seasoning Mix

6 English muffins, split

1 can (16 oz.) OLD EL PASO Refried Beans or OLD EL PASO
    Refried Beans with Green Chilies or OLD EL PASO
    Refried Beans with Sausage

2 cups (8 oz.) shredded Cheddar cheese or Monterey
    Jack cheese

1 can (4 oz.) OLD EL PASO Chopped Green Chilies

1 jar (8 oz.) OLD EL PASO Taco Sauce

Preheat oven to 350°F. Prepare ground beef according to
directions on seasoning mix package; set aside. Heat English
muffins in oven for five minutes. Spread each muffin half with
beans, top with ground beef and cheese. Sprinkle green chilies
over cheese. Place under broiler until heated through and cheese
is melted. Serve with taco sauce. Makes 6 servings.

ENCHILADA MEATBALLS

1½ pounds ground beef

½ pound hot pork sausage

1 package (1¼ oz.) OLD EL PASO Taco Seasoning Mix

1 egg

¼ cup chopped onion

1 can (10 oz.) OLD EL PASO Hot Enchilada Sauce

1 can (10¾ oz.) cream of mushroom soup

1 can (10¾ oz.) tomato soup

1½ cups (6 oz.) shredded sharp Cheddar cheese

Combine ground beef, pork sausage, seasoning mix, egg and
onion; mix well. Shape into 1-inch balls. Place meatballs in a large
skillet and brown on all sides. Drain fat. Combine enchilada sauce,
soups and cheese. Pour over cooked meatballs. Bring to a slow
boil; reduce heat and simmer 20 minutes.

MICROCOOK meatballs one-half at a time on cooking grill or in
2-quart dish, on full power for 10 to 12 minutes or until beef is no
longer pink. Turn dish halfway through cooking time. Drain excess
grease. Pour sauce over cooked meatballs and microcook on full
power for 10 to 12 minutes or until heated through, stirring every
4 minutes.

APPETIZER HOTS

1 pound weiners
1 can (14 oz.) OLD EL PASO Enchilada Sauce
½ cup brown sugar
1½ teaspoons cider vinegar
½ teaspoon Worcestershire sauce

Cut weiners into bite size pieces, about 1-inch in length. Combine enchilada sauce, brown sugar, vinegar and Worcestershire sauce in saucepan. Add hot dogs to sauce, heat to boiling and simmer 15 to 20 minutes uncovered. Place in a fondue pot and keep warm. Serve with toothpicks. Makes about 36 appetizers.

MICROCOOK on high 7 to 8 minutes or until heated through, stirring every two minutes.

MEXI-PEANUTS

¼ cup olive oil
1 package (1¼ oz.) OLD EL PASO Taco Seasoning Mix
1 clove garlic, minced
¼ teaspoon cumin
6 drops liquid hot pepper sauce
16 ounces blanched, salted peanuts

Heat oil in heavy-skillet for 1 minute. Add taco seasoning mix, garlic, cumin and hot pepper sauce stirring constantly. Add peanuts and stir over medium heat about 5 minutes. Store in covered container.

CHEESY SHRIMP DIP

½ cup chopped onion
2 tablespoons vegetable oil
1 can (10 oz.) OLD EL PASO Tomatoes and Green Chilies
1 pound American cheese, cubed
1 can (4½ oz.) cocktail shrimp, drained
  dash cayenne pepper
  OLD EL PASO NACHIPS Tortilla Chips

Saute onion in oil until translucent. Stir in tomatoes and green chilies. Heat to steaming. Add cheese cubes and cook over low heat until cheese is smooth and melted. Stir in shrimp and pepper. Serve warm with NACHIPS.

MICROCOOK uncovered on 50% power for 6 minutes or until heated through. Stir every two minutes.

MEXICAN PUFFS

3 cups buttermilk baking mix

¾ cup cold water

1 pound pork sausage, fried, drained and crumbled

2½ cups (10 oz.) shredded Cheddar cheese

2 tablespoons chopped OLD EL PASO Jalapeno Peppers

Preheat oven to 400°F. Combine buttermilk baking mix and water to make a dough. Add sausage, cheese and peppers to dough. Drop by teaspoonfuls onto a lightly greased baking sheet. Bake for 10 minutes.

NOTE: For a milder puff add ¼ cup chopped green chilies in place of jalapeno peppers.

APPETIZER CHILIES RELLENOS

2 packages (8 oz. each) refrigerator crescent dinner rolls

2 cups (8 oz.) shredded Cheddar cheese

2 cans (4 oz. each) OLD EL PASO Chopped Green Chilies, drained

OLD EL PASO Taco Sauce

Lay crescent rolls flat; overlap at perforated edge. Flatten to ¹⁄₁₆-inch with a lightly floured rolling pin. Cut into 2½-inch circles with a biscuit cutter. Combine cheese and green chilies. Preheat oven to 375°F. Place 1 teaspoon cheese mixture off center of each circle. Fold closest edge over to cover cheese. Fold in both sides, envelope fashion. Roll and place seam-side down on a baking sheet. Bake for 8 to 10 minutes. Serve immediately with taco sauce. Makes 32 miniature chilies rellenos.

NACHOS SUPREME

1 pound ground beef

1 envelope (1¼ oz.) OLD EL PASO Taco Seasoning Mix

1 box (7½ oz.) OLD EL PASO NACHIPS Tortilla Chips

shredded Cheddar cheese

shredded lettuce

OLD EL PASO Taco Sauce

Prepare ground beef according to directions on seasoning mix package. Preheat oven to 400°F. Place NACHIPS on a baking sheet. Top each with 1 tablespoon ground beef mixture and shredded cheese. Bake for 3 minutes or until cheese is melted. Top with shredded lettuce and 1 teaspoon of taco sauce. Serve immediately.

25

BREADS

This cheese-filled bread will bring "ohs and ahs" at a party.

FESTIVE CHEESE LOAF
    2 packages active dry yeast

  2½ teaspoons sugar

    ¼ cup warm water (110°F-115°F)

    1 small can (5.33 fl. oz.) PET Evaporated Milk

    ⅓ cup water

3½-4 cups all-purpose flour

    ½ cup butter, softened

    2 teaspoons salt

    2 pounds (8 cups) shredded Muenster cheese

    1 can (4 oz.) OLD EL PASO Chopped Green Chilies

    1 egg

    2 tablespoons ground coriander

Dissolve yeast and sugar in warm water. Combine evaporated milk and ⅓ cup water. Heat to 110°F. Add to yeast mixture. Slowly beat in flour, butter and salt. Cover and let rise 1 hour or until doubled in size. Roll on floured board into a circle, about 20-inches in diameter. Preheat oven to 400°F. Combine cheese, green chilies, egg and coriander. Place in center of dough. Fold in dough, pleating as you fold, leaving a 2 to 3-inch center of cheese visible. It should now be about 9-inches in diameter. Gently slide greased baking sheet under filled loaf. Cover and let rise 1 hour. Bake for 30 to 35 minutes or until golden brown. Cool 15 minutes before serving. Slice in small wedges to serve. Makes 24 servings.

MEXICAN CORN BREAD
2 packages (8½ oz. each) corn muffin mix

2 cans (4 oz. each) OLD EL PASO Chopped Green
               Chilies, well drained

Preheat oven to 400°F. Prepare corn muffin mix according to package directions. Stir in green chilies. Pour into a 9x9-inch square pan. Bake for 15 to 20 minutes. Makes 6 to 8 servings.

CHILI CORN FRITTERS

1 cup all-purpose flour

2 teaspoons baking powder

½ teaspoon salt

  pepper

1 tablespoon shortening, melted

3 eggs, beaten

½ cup milk

1 teaspoon sugar

1 can (4 oz.) OLD EL PASO Chopped Green Chilies

2 cups cooked corn

  OLD EL PASO Taco Sauce

Combine flour, baking powder, salt and pepper. Stir in shortening and add eggs, milk, sugar, green chilies and corn. Beat well and drop the batter by ¼ cupfuls into deep, hot (375°F) fat and fry until brown. Drain on paper towels. Serve with taco sauce. Makes 4 to 6 servings. Caution: Make sure fat is at 375°F before spooning batter in each time.

Spoon bread is a souffle-like bread served with a spoon and eaten with a fork. This one has Mexican seasonings.

MEXICAN SPOON BREAD WITH GREEN CHILIES

1 cup PET Evaporated Milk

1 cup water

1 cup corn meal

1 tablespoon sugar

1 teaspoon salt

2 tablespoons butter

4 eggs, separated

½ cup (2 oz.) shredded American or Cheddar cheese

1 can (4 oz.) OLD EL PASO Chopped Green Chilies

Heat evaporated milk, water and corn meal in a 2-quart saucepan until thickened, stirring constantly. Remove from heat. Mix in sugar, salt and butter. Cool slightly. Preheat oven to 350°F. Meanwhile, beat egg whites until stiff. Stir cheese, green chilies and egg yolks into hot corn meal mixture. Fold into beaten egg whites. Pour into well-buttered 1½-quart baking dish. Bake for 40 to 45 minutes. Makes 8 servings.

Overleaf: Festive Cheese Loaf

BEEF CHILI CHEESE BRAID

2¾-3 cups all-purpose flour
1 package active dry yeast
¾ cup water
2 tablespoons butter
1 tablespoon sugar
½ teaspoon salt
1 egg

．．．

2 tablespoons butter, melted
½ teaspoon dried fines herbes, crushed
1 can (4 oz.) OLD EL PASO Chopped Green Chilies
½ cup (2 oz.) shredded Swiss cheese
½ cup (2 oz.) snipped thinly sliced smoked beef
dried fines herbes, crushed

In a large mixing bowl, combine 1 cup flour and yeast. In a saucepan, heat water, butter, sugar and salt, just until warm (115°F to 120°F), stirring constantly until butter almost melts. Add liquid to dry ingredients in mixing bowl along with the egg. Beat at low speed of electric mixer for ½ minute, scraping sides of bowl constantly. Beat 3 minutes at high speed. By hand, stir in as much of the remaining flour as you can mix in with a spoon. Knead in enough of the remaining flour to make a moderately stiff dough that is smooth and elastic (about 5 minutes). Cover dough; let rest 10 minutes.

On a lightly floured surface, roll dough to 12x9-inch rectangle. Cut dough lengthwise into three 12x3-inch strips. Brush strips with some of the melted butter; sprinkle with fines herbes. Sprinkle a third of the green chilies, cheese and beef lengthwise down center of each strip. Bring lengthwise edges of each strip together, enclosing filling; pinch all edges together to seal. Place strips side-by-side on a large baking sheet, seam-side down; braid together and secure ends. Cover; place in oven. Turn oven on to 250°F; turn off after one minute. Open oven door slightly; let dough rise until nearly doubled in size (about 30 minutes). Remove from oven; preheat oven to 375°F. Bake for 25 to 30 minutes, or until golden brown and loaf sounds hollow when lightly tapped. Transfer to wire rack; brush loaf with remaining melted butter and sprinkle with additional crushed fines herbes. Serve warm. Makes 1 loaf.

Preceding page: Beef Chili Cheese Braid

MEXICALI BUBBLE LOAF

1 package (13¾ oz.) hot roll mix
¾ cup warm water (110°F-115°F)
1 egg
2 tablespoons OLD EL PASO Taco Seasoning Mix
4-5 tablespoons white corn meal
3-4 tablespoons sesame seed
2 tablespoons finely chopped green pepper
2 tablespoons finely chopped black olives
2 tablespoons finely chopped pimiento, drained
¼ cup butter, melted

In a large mixing bowl, dissolve yeast from hot roll mix in the
warm water; let stand for 3 minutes. Stir in egg. In another bowl,
combine the flour mixture from roll mix and the seasoning mix.
Add to liquid mixture and stir until well mixed. Turn dough out onto
a lightly floured surface; knead 5 minutes or until dough is smooth
and elastic. Place dough in greased bowl; turn once to grease
surface. Cover; let rise in warm place until doubled in size, (about
1½ hours). In a small bowl, combine corn meal and sesame seed;
set aside. In another small bowl, combine the chopped green
pepper, olives and pimiento. Turn dough out on a well-floured
surface, kneading lightly until no longer sticky. Shape dough into
24 balls. Dip each ball in the melted butter, then the corn meal
mixture to coat. Arrange 12 of the balls in the bottom of a greased
6½ cup metal ring mold. Sprinkle the green pepper mixture evenly
over balls in mold. Place the remaining balls over filling in mold.
Cover and let rise in a warm place until doubled in size, (about
1 hour). Cover with foil and bake in preheated 375°F oven for
15 minutes. Remove foil and bake 5 to 10 minutes more or until
golden brown and loaf sounds hollow when lightly tapped.
Immediately turn out of pan; cool slightly on rack. Serve warm.
Makes 1 loaf.

This bread is excellent for sandwiches, toast or served sliced with any meal.

RAISED MEXICAN CORN BREAD

2 packages active dry yeast

1 cup corn meal, plus some for pans

½ teaspoon baking soda

1 cup buttermilk

1 medium onion, finely chopped

½ cup vegetable oil

1 tablespoon salt

1 tablespoon sugar

2 eggs

1½ cups (6 oz.) shredded sharp Cheddar cheese

1 cup cream style corn

1 can (4 oz.) OLD EL PASO Chopped Green Chilies

6½ - 7 cups all-purpose flour

¼ cup butter, melted

In a large bowl, mix yeast, 1 cup corn meal and baking soda; set aside. In saucepan, heat buttermilk, onion, oil, salt and sugar until very warm (120°F to 130°F). Stir into corn meal mixture. Beat in eggs, cheese, corn and green chilies. Stir in 5 cups flour, 1 cup at a time until well mixed. Turn out on lightly floured surface; knead in enough remaining flour until dough is smooth and elastic. Place in greased bowl; turn to grease top. Cover and let rise in warm, draft-free place until doubled in size, (about 1 to 2 hours). Grease two 9x5x3-inch or 10x4x3-inch loaf pans; dust lightly with corn meal. Divide dough in half. On lightly floured surface, roll out each to 18x8-inch rectangle and roll into loaf. Place seam-side down in pan. Brush each loaf with butter. Cover; let rise in warm, draft-free place until doubled in size, (30 to 45 minutes). Bake in preheated 400°F oven for 25 to 30 minutes. Remove from pans to rack. Brush with remaining butter. Cool completely. May be tightly wrapped and frozen. Makes 2 loaves.

Following page: Bean and Sausage Tostadas

BEANS AND RICE

BEAN AND HAM TACOS

2 cups diced cooked ham

1 tablespoon butter

1 can (16 oz.) OLD EL PASO Refried Beans or OLD EL PASO
     Refried Beans with Green Chilies or OLD EL PASO
     Refried Beans with Sausage

½ cup sour cream

½ teaspoon chili powder

12 OLD EL PASO Taco Shells

1 cup (4 oz.) shredded Swiss cheese

2 cups shredded lettuce

1 medium tomato, chopped

  OLD EL PASO Taco Sauce

Preheat oven to 350°F. Brown ham in butter in medium skillet. Stir in beans, sour cream and chili powder. Cook over low heat, stirring constantly until heated through. Place taco shells on baking sheet and heat for 5 to 7 minutes. Spoon ham filling into taco shells. Top with cheese, lettuce and tomato. Serve with taco sauce. Makes 12 tacos.

BEAN AND SAUSAGE TOSTADAS

1 can (15 oz.) OLD EL PASO Refried Beans with Sausage

6 OLD EL PASO Tostada Shells

  shredded lettuce

  chopped tomatoes

  shredded Cheddar cheese

  OLD EL PASO Taco Sauce

Preheat oven to 350°F. Heat beans with sausage in a saucepan over medium heat, until steaming. Place tostada shells on a baking sheet. Warm in oven for 5 to 7 minutes. Spread each tostada shell with ¼ cup beans. Top with lettuce, tomato, cheese and taco sauce, as desired. Makes 6 tostadas.

A seasoned rice like this is often part of the Mexican menu.

GREEN RICE

3 cups cooked rice

1 cup chopped fresh parsley

½ cup (2 oz.) shredded Cheddar cheese

⅓ cup chopped onion

1 can (4 oz.) OLD EL PASO Chopped Green Chilies

1 clove garlic, minced

1 tall can (13 fl. oz.) PET Evaporated Milk

2 eggs, beaten

½ cup vegetable oil

1 teaspoon salt

½ teaspoon pepper

   juice and grated rind of a small lemon

   paprika

Mix rice, parsley, cheese, onion, green chilies and garlic in a greased 2-quart baking dish. Preheat oven to 350°F. Blend together evaporated milk, eggs, oil, salt, pepper and lemon. Mix into rice. Sprinkle with paprika. Bake for 45 minutes, or until knife inserted 1-inch from edge comes out clean. Makes 6 to 8 servings.

This is an easy casserole with piquant seasonings.

CHILI GRITS

1½ cups quick grits

1½ teaspoons salt

  6 cups boiling water

 ½ cup butter

 2 cups (8 oz.) shredded Cheddar cheese

 2 tablespoons finely chopped OLD EL PASO Jalapeno Peppers

 3 eggs, beaten

 1 can (10¾ oz.) cream of chicken soup

 ½ teaspoon salt

Preheat oven to 325°F. Cook the grits in boiling, salted water for 8 minutes. Add butter, cheese, peppers, eggs, soup and salt; mix well and spread in a greased 2-quart baking dish. Bake for 1 to 1½-hours, covering for first 45 minutes, then remove cover and continue baking until lightly browned. Makes 8 servings.

The delicious flavor belies the ease of preparation.

QUICK MEXICAN RICE

4 cups cooked rice (cooked in chicken broth)
1 pint (2 cups) sour cream
1 can (4 oz.) OLD EL PASO Chopped Green Chilies
1 cup (4 oz.) shredded Monterey Jack cheese

Cook rice according to package directions, substituting chicken broth for the water. Mix cooked rice with sour cream. Preheat oven to 350°F. Put ½ of cooked rice in 2-quart greased baking dish; layer ½ of the green chilies and ½ of the cheese. Repeat layers. Bake for 30 minutes. Makes 6 to 8 servings.

RED RICE

1 medium onion
1 clove garlic
½ teaspoon salt
1 tablespoon bacon drippings
1 can (10 oz.) OLD EL PASO Tomatoes and Green Chilies
½ cup chicken broth
½ teaspoon chili powder
⅛ teaspoon ground cumin
1 cup instant rice

Cut onion in half. Finely chop one half. Cut the other half in very thin slices. Mash garlic with salt to make a paste. Heat bacon drippings in a medium saucepan. Add chopped onion and garlic paste. Cook and stir until onion is translucent. Add tomatoes and green chilies, chicken broth, chili powder and cumin. Bring mixture to a boil. Stir in rice and sliced onion. Cover and let stand over very low heat 15 to 20 minutes or until liquid is absorbed. Makes 4 servings.

Following page: Flautas

BASICS OF MEXICAN COOKERY

Flauta means "flute" in Spanish. Flautas are simply tortillas rolled around a spicy meat filling and fried crisp.

FLAUTAS

1 pound ground beef
1 envelope (1¼ oz.) OLD EL PASO Taco Seasoning Mix
1 jar (16 oz.) OLD EL PASO Taco Sauce, divided usage
24 OLD EL PASO Corn Tortillas or flour tortillas, 6-inch

Brown ground beef in medium skillet. Drain fat. Stir in seasoning mix and 1 cup of taco sauce. Simmer 5 minutes. If using flour tortillas, eliminate frying stage. For each flauta, dip 2 tortillas in hot oil for a few seconds on each side to soften. Drain on paper towels. Lay the tortillas flat and overlapping about 2 inches. Spoon 1 to 2 tablespoons of meat filling lengthwise near 1 edge of overlapping tortillas. Roll tightly around filling and secure with toothpicks. Fry in 1-inch of hot oil until the flauta is crisp. Drain on paper towels. Serve immediately with taco sauce. Makes 12 flautas, 2 to 3 to a serving.

BEEF TACOS

- 1 pound ground beef
- 1 medium onion, chopped
- 1 clove garlic, minced
- 1 envelope (1¼ oz.) OLD EL PASO Taco Seasoning Mix
- ¾ cup water
- 12 OLD EL PASO Taco Shells
- 2 tomatoes, chopped
- 1 cup (4 oz.) shredded sharp Cheddar cheese
  shredded lettuce
  OLD EL PASO Taco Sauce

Brown ground beef, onion and garlic in medium skillet. Drain fat. Stir in seasoning mix and water. Heat to boiling. Reduce heat and simmer, uncovered, 15 to 20 minutes, stirring occasionally. Preheat oven to 350°F. Arrange taco shells on baking sheet. Warm in oven for 5 to 7 minutes. Fill each of the taco shells with some of the meat mixture, tomatoes, cheese and lettuce. Serve with taco sauce. Makes 12 tacos.

Overleaf: Taco Bar

BEEF AND BEAN TOSTADAS

1 pound ground beef

1 envelope (1¼ oz.) OLD EL PASO Taco Seasoning Mix

12 OLD EL PASO Tostada Shells

2 cans (16 oz. each) OLD EL PASO Refried Beans or OLD
EL PASO Refried Beans with Green Chilies or OLD
EL PASO Refried Beans with Sausage, heated

shredded lettuce

diced tomatoes

shredded Cheddar cheese

OLD EL PASO Taco Sauce

Prepare ground beef according to directions on seasoning mix
package. Preheat oven to 350°F. Place tostada shells on baking
sheet. Warm in oven for 5 to 7 minutes. Spread each tostada shell
with ¼ cup beans. Top with 1 to 2 tablespoons ground beef
mixture, shredded lettuce, tomatoes, cheese and taco sauce.
Makes 12 tostadas.

NACHOS

1 box (7½ oz.) OLD EL PASO NACHIPS Tortilla Chips

1 can (16 oz.) OLD EL PASO Refried Beans or OLD EL PASO Refried Beans with Green Chilies or OLD EL PASO Refried Beans with Sausage

1 can (4 oz.) OLD EL PASO Chopped Green Chilies or 1 jar (11½ oz.) OLD EL PASO Jalapeno Slices

2½ cups (10 oz.) shredded Cheddar or Monterey Jack cheese

Spread tortilla chips on a large baking sheet. Top each with beans and a few green chilies or a slice of jalapeno pepper. Sprinkle each with a tablespoon of cheese. Place under broiler until cheese melts, about 2 to 3 minutes. Serve immediately.

MICROCOOK on full power until cheese is melted, about 2-3 minutes. Time will vary with the number of nachos prepared.

QUESADILLAS

2 cans (4 oz. each) OLD EL PASO Whole Green Chilies

8 ounces Cheddar cheese or Monterey Jack cheese (cut into 6 strips, 4 x ½ x ½-inch)

6 flour tortillas, 8-inch

1 jar (8 oz.) OLD EL PASO Taco Sauce

Slit chilies; remove seeds and ribs. Wrap each piece of cheese with a chili. Place chili-wrapped cheese in center of tortilla. Fold tortilla in half over chili and insert toothpick to secure. Fry in 1-inch of hot oil until crisp, turning occasionally. Drain on paper towels. Serve immediately with taco sauce. Makes 6 quesadillas.

Chim-mee-chan-gas are a variation of burritos. They're simply fried rather than baked.

CHIMICHANGAS

1 pound ground beef
1 can (10 oz.) OLD EL PASO Tomatoes and Green Chilies
1 envelope (1¼ oz.) OLD EL PASO Taco Seasoning Mix
12 flour tortillas, 8-inch
3 cups shredded lettuce
2 cups (8 oz.) shredded Cheddar cheese
¼ cup sliced green onions
1½ cups OLD EL PASO Taco Sauce

Brown ground beef in medium skillet. Drain fat. Stir in tomatoes and green chilies and seasoning mix. Simmer 5 minutes. Spoon ¼ cup of meat mixture along one edge of tortilla. Fold nearest edge over to cover filling. Fold in both sides, envelope fashion. Roll and secure with toothpicks. Fry in 1-inch of hot oil until golden, turning as necessary. Drain on paper towels. Keep warm while preparing others. Before serving, top each chimichanga with ⅓ cup lettuce, ¼ cup cheese, 1 teaspoon green onions and 2 tablespoons taco sauce. Serve immediately. Makes 12 chimichangas.

Following page: Chimichangas

HEARTY BEEFY ENCHILADAS

1½ cups cooked shredded beef

2 cups (8 oz.) shredded sharp Cheddar cheese,
    divided usage

¾ cup chopped onion

1 can (4 oz.) OLD EL PASO Chopped Green Chilies

1 can (10¾ oz.) cream of mushroom soup

1 can (10¾ oz.) tomato soup

1 can (10 oz.) OLD EL PASO Hot Enchilada Sauce

12 OLD EL PASO Corn Tortillas

Combine beef, ½ cup cheese, onion and green chilies; set aside.
Combine soups and enchilada sauce. Fry tortillas in hot oil to
soften, a few seconds on each side. Drain on paper towels.
Preheat oven to 350°F. Top each tortilla with one heaping
tablespoon of meat mixture. Roll and place seam-side down in a
13x9-inch baking dish. Pour sauce over and top with remaining
cheese. Bake for 25 to 30 minutes. Makes 6 servings.

MICROCOOK enchiladas on 70% power for 14 to 16 minutes or
until heated through. Turn twice during cooking time.

SOUTH OF THE BORDER ENCHILADAS

1½ pounds ground beef

1 package (1¼ oz.) OLD EL PASO Taco Seasoning Mix

1 can (12 oz.) tomato paste

1 cup water

½ cup chopped onion

1 teaspoon salt

12 flour tortillas, 8-inch

1 jar (8 oz.) pasteurized process cheese spread

1 can (4 oz.) OLD EL PASO Chopped Green Chilies

Brown ground beef in large skillet. Drain well. Stir in seasoning
mix, tomato paste, water, onion and salt. Simmer for 15 to 20
minutes; stirring occasionally until liquid is reduced. Preheat oven
to 350°F. Spoon 2 to 3 tablespoons meat mixture on each tortilla.
Roll tightly and place in a 13x9-inch baking dish. Spread cheese
over top of enchiladas. Sprinkle with green chilies. Top with
remaining meat mixture. Bake for 25 to 30 minutes. Remove with
spatula and serve immediately. Makes 12 enchiladas.

MICROCOOK on full power for 10 to 12 minutes or until heated
through. Turn once during cooking time.

BURRITOS

12 flour tortillas, 10-inch

1 large onion, chopped

2 tablespoons butter

2 cans (16 oz. each) OLD EL PASO Refried Beans or
OLD EL PASO Refried Beans with Green Chilies
or OLD EL PASO Refried Beans with Sausage

2 large tomatoes, chopped

3 cups (12 oz.) shredded Cheddar cheese

2 cups shredded lettuce

OLD EL PASO Taco Sauce or OLD EL PASO Tomatoes
and Green Chilies

Preheat oven to 350°F. Wrap stack of tortillas tightly in foil; heat in oven for 15 minutes. Cook onion in butter until translucent. Add beans; cook and stir until heated through. Lightly salt tomatoes. Spoon about ⅓ cup bean mixture onto each tortilla near one edge. Top with cheese, lettuce, tomato and 2 tablespoons of taco sauce or tomatoes and green chilies. Fold nearest edge over to cover filling. Fold in both sides envelope fashion. Roll and arrange on baking sheet. Bake for 15 minutes or until heated through. Serve with taco sauce or tomatoes and green chilies. Makes 12 burritos.

CHILIES RELLENOS

6 OLD EL PASO Whole Green Chilies

8 ounces Cheddar cheese (cut into 6 strips, 3x½x½-inch)

6 tablespoons all-purpose flour, divided usage

6 eggs, separated

¼ teaspoon salt

shortening or cooking oil

OLD EL PASO Taco Sauce

Slit chilies lengthwise; seed, and drain on paper towel. Stuff chilies with cheese; roll in 3 tablespoons flour. In medium mixing bowl beat egg whites until stiff but not dry. Set aside. Add remaining flour and salt to egg yolks; beat until thick and lemon colored. Fold into egg whites. Dip chilies in egg batter, covering well. Deep fry in 400°F oil until golden brown all over. Drain on paper towels. Serve immediately with taco sauce. Makes 6 chilies rellenos.

Overleaf: South of the Border Enchiladas

MAIN DISHES
Cheese

Flavorful and colorful, excellent for brunch.

COTTAGE ENCHILADAS

2 cans (4 oz. each) OLD EL PASO Chopped Green Chilies

4 cups (16 oz.) shredded sharp American cheese,
    divided usage

1 carton (12 oz.) cream-style cottage cheese

1 clove garlic, minced

½ teaspoon coriander

½ teaspoon salt

⅛ teaspoon pepper

12 OLD EL PASO Corn Tortillas or flour tortillas, 6-inch
    or 8-inch

1 cup sour cream

1 can (10 oz.) OLD EL PASO Green Chili Enchilada Sauce

Preheat oven to 350°F. Mix together green chilies, 2 cups
American cheese, cottage cheese, garlic, coriander, salt and
pepper. Set aside. If using flour tortillas, eliminate frying stage.
Fry tortillas in hot oil a few seconds on each side until limp.
Drain on paper towels. Spoon one heaping tablespoon of cheese
mixture on each tortilla. Roll and place seam-side down in a
13x9-inch baking dish. Spoon remaining cheese mixture in a
row over center of enchiladas. Combine sour cream and
enchilada sauce. Pour over tortillas. Top with remaining
shredded cheese. Bake for 25 to 30 minutes until bubbly.
Makes 6 servings.

MICROCOOK enchiladas on 70% power for 14 to 16 minutes or
until heated through. Turn twice during cooking time.

Preceding page: Chili Cheese Strata

CHEESE TACOS

½ cup chopped onion

2 tablespoons butter

1 can (10 oz.) OLD EL PASO Tomatoes and Green Chilies

1 teaspoon dried oregano, crushed

8 ounces Monterey Jack or Cheddar cheese

12 OLD EL PASO Taco Shells

1 avocado, peeled and cut in 12 wedges

shredded lettuce

diced tomato

1 cup sour cream

Cook onion in butter until translucent. Stir in tomatoes and green chilies and oregano. Simmer 15 minutes, keep warm. Preheat oven to 350°F. Cut cheese into 12 strips. Place one cheese strip in each taco shell. Arrange on baking sheet. Bake, uncovered, for 7 to 8 minutes or until cheese starts to melt. Top cheese with a spoonful of tomatoes and chilies mixture, an avocado slice, lettuce, tomato and a dollop of sour cream. Makes 12 tacos.

CHILIES RELLENOS BAKE

2 cans (4 oz. each) OLD EL PASO Whole Green Chilies

8 ounces Cheddar cheese, (cut into 10 strips, 3x½x½-inch)

1 can (10 oz.) refrigerated biscuits

3 eggs, separated

¼ teaspoon salt

OLD EL PASO Taco Sauce

Slit chilies lengthwise to make 10 pieces. Remove seeds and ribs. Drain on paper towels. Wrap each piece of cheese with a chili. Separate dough into 10 biscuits. Press or roll each to a 5-inch circle. Preheat oven to 375°F. Place 1 chili-wrapped cheese piece on each biscuit. Fold dough over cheese and pinch to seal. Form a finger-like roll; place seam-side down on greased baking sheet. Bake for 10 to 12 minutes. Meanwhile, beat egg whites until stiff. Fold in slightly beaten egg yolks just until blended. Fold in salt. Spoon egg mixture over each partially baked rellenos, covering each completely. Continue baking 12 to 15 minutes or until golden brown. Serve with taco sauce. Makes 10 chilies rellenos.

CHEESE ENCHILADAS

   1 medium onion, chopped
   1 small green pepper, chopped
   1 cup chopped mushrooms
   5 tablespoons shortening, divided usage
   1 can (10 oz.) OLD EL PASO Mild Enchilada Sauce
   1 can (10¾ oz.) cream of mushroom soup
   1 can (4 oz.) OLD EL PASO Chopped Green Chilies
   ½ teaspoon garlic salt
12 OLD EL PASO Corn Tortillas
   2 cups (8 oz.) shredded Cheddar cheese, divided usage

In a small frying pan, saute onion, green pepper and mushrooms in 2 tablespoons shortening. Set aside. Preheat oven to 350°F. Mix enchilada sauce, mushroom soup, green chilies and garlic salt in a small mixing bowl. Combine ½ of this mixture with the sauteed onion, green pepper and mushrooms. Reserve the remaining half and 1 cup cheese. Fry tortillas in remaining 3 tablespoons heated shortening, one at a time for 5 seconds on each side. Drain on paper towels. Fill each with cheese and enchilada sauce/sauteed mixture. Roll and place seam-side down in a 13x9-inch baking dish. Pour remaining enchilada sauce mixture over. Top with remaining cheese and bake for 15 minutes. Makes 12 enchiladas.

MICROCOOK enchiladas on 70% power 12-14 minutes or until heated through. Turn twice during cooking time.

Preceding page: Cheese Enchiladas

This is a good accompaniment for Stuffed Flank Steak or Beef Spinach Roulade.

CHILI POTATO PUFFS

6 small potatoes, peeled

1 tablespoon butter

3 tablespoons PET Evaporated Milk

1 teaspoon salt

1 egg

1 can (4 oz.) OLD EL PASO Chopped Green Chilies

12 1-inch cubes of cheese

    parsley

    tomato

Preheat oven to 450°F. Cook potatoes in boiling salted water until tender. Mash well with butter, evaporated milk, salt and egg. Stir in green chilies. Beat well. Using an ice cream scoop, scoop out potatoes onto a well-greased baking sheet. With handle of teaspoon make a hollow place in the scoop and fill with a cube of cheese. Bake for 20 minutes or until golden brown. Serve puffs sprinkled with chopped parsley and garnished with slices of tomato, if desired. Makes 12 servings.

MEXI-CHEESE SALAD

1 cup small elbow macaroni

1 teaspoon vegetable oil

1 cup frozen peas

2 tablespoons finely chopped red onion

1 cup small-curd cottage cheese

½ cup mayonnaise

½ cup diced cooked carrots, drained

1 can (4 oz.) OLD EL PASO Chopped Green Chilies

½ teaspoon salt

    lettuce leaves

    tomato wedges

    OLD EL PASO Taco Sauce

Cook macaroni in boiling salted water until tender, 8 to 10 minutes. Drain and cool. Place in a medium bowl. Toss with oil. Add peas, onion, cottage cheese, mayonnaise, carrots, green chilies and salt. Toss gently but thoroughly. Chill. Line 6 salad plates with lettuce leaves. Spoon macaroni mixture onto leaves. Garnish with tomato wedges. Serve with taco sauce. Makes 6 servings.

Great make-ahead buffet or brunch dish.

CHILI CHEESE STRATA

8 slices day-old bread

6 ounces sharp American or Swiss cheese, sliced

1 can (4 oz.) OLD EL PASO Chopped Green Chilies,
    well drained

4 eggs

1 tall can (13 fl. oz.) PET Evaporated Milk

¾ cup water

¼ cup finely chopped onion

1½ teaspoons salt

½ teaspoon prepared mustard

   dash pepper

   paprika

Trim crusts from 4 slices bread. Halve slices diagonally to make 8 triangles; set aside. Arrange trimmings and remaining 4 slices on bottom of 9-inch square baking dish. Place cheese slices on top. Sprinkle with green chilies. Arrange bread triangles in 2 rows over cheese. Beat eggs. Stir in evaporated milk, water, onion, salt, mustard and pepper. Pour over bread. Sprinkle with paprika. Cover and let stand 1 hour at room temperature or several hours in the refrigerator. Bake uncovered in preheated 325°F oven until knife inserted in center comes out clean, about 1 hour. Let stand 5 minutes before serving. Makes 6 servings.

MAIN DISHES
Eggs

Traditional Mexican breakfast dish.

HUEVOS RANCHEROS

6 OLD EL PASO Corn Tortillas or flour tortillas

½ cup chopped onion

1 clove garlic, minced

2 tablespoons vegetable oil

1⅔ cups (14 oz.) canned tomatoes

2 cans (4 oz. each) OLD EL PASO Chopped Green Chilies

¾ teaspoon salt, divided usage

6 eggs

⅛ teaspoon pepper

1 cup (4 oz.) shredded Cheddar cheese

¼ cup butter, melted

Fry tortillas in 1-inch of hot oil until crispy. Line a jelly-roll pan with tortillas. Cook onion and garlic in 2 tablespoons oil until tender. Stir in tomatoes, green chilies and ½ teaspoon salt. Pour over tortillas. Preheat oven to 350°F. Carefully break eggs, one on top of each tortilla. Sprinkle remaining salt, pepper and cheese over eggs. Dribble butter over; cover. Bake for 15 minutes. Serve immediately. Makes 6 servings.

Preceding page: Huevos Rancheros

Omelet with an unusual filling.

SAUCY OMELET

1 cup peeled, cubed eggplant

½ cup zucchini slices

1 can (4 oz.) OLD EL PASO Chopped Green Chilies,
 well drained

4 tablespoons butter, divided usage

½ cup OLD EL PASO Taco Sauce

6 eggs, slightly beaten

2 tablespoons water

¼ teaspoon salt

 dash of pepper

Saute eggplant, zucchini and green chilies in 2 tablespoons butter until crisp-tender. Stir in taco sauce; heat. Melt remaining butter in 10-inch skillet or omelet pan over medium high heat, just until hot enough to sizzle a drop of water. Combine eggs, water, salt and pepper; pour into skillet. As egg mixture sets, lift edges slightly with spatula to allow uncooked portion to flow underneath. When egg mixture is set, but top is still moist, place half of vegetable mixture on half of omelet. Overlap omelet and invert onto serving plate. Spoon remaining vegetable mixture over omelet. Makes 4 servings.

Colorful dish with zesty flavor.

EGGS SONORA

6 flour tortillas, 6-inch

1 dozen eggs, scrambled

1 cup (4 oz.) shredded Cheddar cheese

10 slices bacon, cooked, drained and crumbled

1 medium onion, finely chopped

1 can (4 oz.) OLD EL PASO Chopped Green Chilies

1 cup guacamole (see recipe page 19)

¼ cup sliced black olives

 sour cream

1 jar (8 oz.) OLD EL PASO Taco Sauce

Preheat oven to 350°F. Wrap tortillas in foil; bake for 15 minutes. Arrange tortillas on baking sheet. Layer eggs, cheese, bacon, onion, green chilies, guacamole and olives evenly on each warm tortilla. Warm in oven for 5 minutes longer. Top with a dollop of sour cream. Serve with taco sauce. Makes 6 servings.

Spicy Mexican flavors give this omelet a new taste.

CHILI OMELET

2 eggs

2 tablespoons OLD EL PASO Chopped Green Chilies, drained

¼ cup (1 oz.) shredded Cheddar cheese

2 tablespoons sliced black olives

⅛ teaspoon salt

dash of pepper

1 tablespoon butter

1 tablespoon sour cream

Beat eggs with fork. Add green chilies, cheese, olives, salt and pepper; mix with a fork until blended. In an 8-inch skillet or omelet pan, heat the butter just until hot enough to sizzle a drop of water. Add egg mixture; cook over medium heat. As egg mixture sets, lift edges slightly with spatula to allow uncooked portion to flow underneath. Remove from heat. Spoon sour cream filling across center. Overlap omelet and invert onto serving plate. Makes 1 omelet.

MEXI-BRUNCH EGGS

2 large baking potatoes, peeled

½ pound bulk pork sausage

½ cup finely chopped onion

1 can (4 oz.) OLD EL PASO Chopped Green Chilies

4 eggs

1 avocado, peeled, seeded and sliced

cilantro or parsley sprigs, if desired

OLD EL PASO Taco Sauce

Dice potatoes into ¼-inch cubes. In a large skillet, cook and mash sausage until lightly browned. Add diced potatoes, onion and green chilies. Cover and cook over medium heat until potatoes are tender; about 15 minutes. Remove lid. With the back of a large spoon, press 4 indentations in mixture. Break an egg into each indentation. Cover and cook until eggs are set; about 5 minutes. To serve, garnish with avocado slices and cilantro or parsley sprigs, if desired. Serve with taco sauce.
Makes 4 servings.

Overleaf: Eggs Sonora

A quick and easy meatless main dish.

TORTILLA HASH

6 OLD EL PASO Corn Tortillas

2 tablespoons vegetable oil

6 eggs, slightly beaten

1 teaspoon salt

1 can (10 oz.) OLD EL PASO Mild Enchilada Sauce

1½ cups (6 oz.) Monterey Jack or Mozzarella cheese, divided usage

½ cup water

¼ cup sliced green onions, divided usage

Tear tortillas into 1½-inch pieces. Fry tortilla pieces in 1 inch hot oil until crisp and golden. Remove with slotted spoon. Reserve 2 tablespoons oil in skillet; return tortilla pieces to skillet. Stir in eggs and salt. Cook and stir until tortilla pieces are coated and eggs are set. Stir in enchilada sauce, 1 cup cheese, water and half of onion. Simmer uncovered for 15 minutes. Spoon into serving dish. Top with remaining cheese and onion.
Makes 4 servings.

Spicy scrambled eggs served in taco shells.

TACO SCRAMBLER

4 OLD EL PASO Taco Shells

¼ cup chopped green onions

2 tablespoons butter

4 eggs, beaten

¼ cup milk

¼ cup chopped tomato

3 tablespoons OLD EL PASO Chopped Green Chilies

½ teaspoon salt

1 jar (8 oz.) pasteurized process cheese spread, heated

OLD EL PASO Taco Sauce

Preheat oven to 350°F. Arrange taco shells on baking sheet, warm in oven for 5 to 7 minutes. Saute onion in butter until translucent. Add eggs, milk, tomato, green chilies and salt. Cook, stirring occasionally, until eggs are set. Spoon into taco shells. Top with cheese spread and taco sauce. Makes 4 tacos.

Preceding page: Taco Scrambler

Good make-ahead brunch casserole.

SAUSAGE AND CHEESE CASSEROLE

½ pound hot, bulk pork sausage

½ cup chopped onion

2 cans (4 oz. each) OLD EL PASO Chopped Green Chilies,
    divided usage

6 eggs, slightly beaten

⅓ cup PET Evaporated Milk

¼ teaspoon salt

1 box (7½ oz.) OLD EL PASO NACHIPS Tortilla Chips,
    divided usage

2 cups (8 oz.) shredded mild Cheddar cheese,
    divided usage

½ cup chopped tomatoes

Brown sausage in medium skillet; drain, reserving 1 tablespoon
fat. Add onion; cook until translucent. Stir in 1 can of the green
chilies. Remove from skillet and set aside. Preheat oven to 350°F.
In reserved fat, cook eggs, evaporated milk and salt, stirring
occasionally until set. In an 11 x 7-inch baking dish, place
one layer of NACHIPS, sausage mixture, half of the cheese,
additional layer of NACHIPS, egg mixture, remaining cheese and
green chilies. Bake for 15 minutes. Garnish with chopped tomatoes.
Makes 6 to 8 servings.

Can be cut into tiny squares for appetizers or larger squares
for a luncheon dish.

CHILI SQUARES

1 can (10 oz.) OLD EL PASO Whole Green Chilies

1 cup polish sausage, sliced then halved

6 eggs

2 cups (8 oz.) shredded Cheddar cheese

2 cups (8 oz.) shredded Mozzarella cheese

¼ teaspoon salt

   OLD EL PASO Taco Sauce

Preheat oven to 350°F. Remove seeds and ribs from chilies and
lay flat in a well-greased 9-inch square baking dish. Place meat
on chilies. Whip eggs until foamy and combine with cheeses and
salt. Pour this over meat. Bake covered for 30 minutes. Lower
oven to 250°F, uncover, and bake 30 minutes longer. Cut into
small squares. Serve with taco sauce. Makes 4 to 6 servings.

MAIN DISHES
Fish

This combination always brings raves from tasters.

SHRIMP CHILI QUICHE

1 PET-RITZ Regular Pie Crust Shell, thawed

2 eggs

1 small can (5.33 fl. oz.) PET Evaporated Milk

2 tablespoons flour

¾ teaspoon garlic salt

½ cup (2 oz.) shredded Cheddar cheese

½ cup (2 oz.) shredded Monterey Jack cheese

½ cup chopped onion

1 can (4 oz.) OLD EL PASO Chopped Green Chilies

1 can (4½ oz.) deveined medium shrimp, drained

Preheat oven and baking sheet to 450°F. Partially bake pie shell about 6 minutes. Remove from oven. Reduce oven temperature to 350°F. Beat together eggs, evaporated milk, flour and garlic salt. (Mixture need not be smooth.) Stir in cheeses, onion and green chilies. Pour into pie shell. Spread shrimp on top of custard mixture. Bake on preheated baking sheet, until knife inserted in center comes out clean, about 35 to 40 minutes. Cool 15 minutes before serving. Makes 6 servings.

Preceding page: Shrimp Chili Quiche with Chili Coleslaw

BAKED SCALLOPS IN CHEESE SAUCE

½ cup dry white wine

2 teaspoons chopped onion

2 pounds sea scallops, cut in half crosswise

2 tablespoons fresh bread crumbs

1½ cups milk, divided usage

6 tablespoons butter

6 tablespoons flour

¼ teaspoon paprika

¼ teaspoon nutmeg

¼ teaspoon cayenne pepper

1½ teaspoons salt

¼ teaspoon ground white pepper

½ cup plus 2 tablespoons shredded Muenster cheese, divided usage

1 can (4 oz.) OLD EL PASO Chopped Green Chilies

2 hard cooked eggs, sliced

In a large saucepan, combine wine and onion, bring to a boil over medium heat. Reduce heat and simmer for 3 minutes. Add scallops, cover and simmer over low heat for 5 minutes or until the scallops become firm and opaque. Drain the scallops and reserve ½ cup cooking liquid. Set scallops and liquid aside. Preheat the oven to 350°F. In a small bowl, soak the bread crumbs in 2 tablespoons of milk. Melt butter over moderate heat in a 2 to 3-quart saucepan. Reduce heat and add flour, stirring constantly for one minute. Then slowly stir in ½ cup of reserved cooking liquid and remaining milk. Cook over medium heat, stirring constantly until the sauce thickens and comes to a boil. Add bread crumbs, paprika, nutmeg, cayenne pepper, salt and white pepper. Stir until well blended. Add cheese and the green chilies and cook for a minute, stirring constantly. Drain scallops on paper towel and add to mixture. Lightly butter a 2-quart baking dish and arrange hard cooked eggs on the bottom. Spoon in scallop mixture and smooth the surface with a spatula. Sprinkle the top with the remaining 2 tablespoons of cheese. Bake for 20 minutes, or until the mixture bubbles and lightly browns on top. Serve at once. Makes 6 to 8 servings.

PUEBLA-STYLE LOBSTER

1 tablespoon salt, divided usage
2 pounds lobster tails
½ cup plus 1 tablespoon butter, divided usage
1 onion, chopped
2 cloves garlic, minced
2 carrots, sliced and cooked
2 bay leaves
½ teaspoon marjoram
½ teaspoon thyme
½ teaspoon nutmeg
1 teaspoon pepper
⅓ cup brandy, warmed
1 can (10 oz.) OLD EL PASO Tomatoes and Green Chilies
2 tablespoons chopped fresh parsley
  hot cooked rice

Add 2 teaspoons salt to 1½-quarts of water and bring to a boil. Drop lobster into boiling water. Simmer for 5 minutes. Remove from heat; let stand about 15 minutes. Drain and cool. Remove cooked meat from the shells and cut in slices. Saute over low heat in ½ cup butter: lobster, onion, garlic, carrots, bay leaves, marjoram, thyme, nutmeg, pepper and remaining salt. When the lobster takes on a reddish color, remove from heat. Pour brandy over mixture and ignite. Let flame until alcohol burns off. Add tomatoes and green chilies, remaining butter and simmer for 5 minutes. Sprinkle with parsley and serve on a bed of rice. Makes 6 servings.

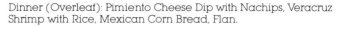
Dinner (Overleaf): Pimiento Cheese Dip with Nachips, Veracruz Shrimp with Rice, Mexican Corn Bread, Flan.

VERACRUZ SHRIMP

 1 pound fresh medium shrimp
 1 large green pepper
 3 tablespoons vegetable oil, divided usage
 1 small onion, chopped
 1 can (4 oz.) OLD EL PASO Chopped Green Chilies
 1 jar (16 oz.) OLD EL PASO Taco Sauce
 2 medium tomatoes, chopped
12 pimiento stuffed olives
1½ teaspoons capers
 ¼ teaspoon cumin
 1 bay leaf
 1 teaspoon salt
 ½ teaspoon sugar
   lime juice
   hot cooked rice

Peel shrimp and remove veins; set aside. Cut green pepper
into 1½ x ½-inch strips. Heat 1 tablespoon oil in a large skillet. Add
green pepper and onion. Cook until onion is translucent. Add
green chilies, taco sauce, tomatoes, olives, capers, cumin, bay
leaf, salt and sugar. Bring to a boil. Reduce heat and simmer
for 10 minutes. Heat 2 tablespoons of oil in a large skillet. Add
shrimp. Cook over medium heat stirring constantly about 3 minutes
or until shrimp turns pink. Sprinkle a few drops of lime juice over
shrimp. Add sauce. Cook 2 minutes longer. Serve immediately
over hot rice. Makes 4 servings.

In this classic Mexican dish, the fish "cooks," or turns white, from marinating in lime juice, or lemon juice.

SEVICHE

1 pound white fish, cut in small cubes
   lime or lemon juice
½ medium onion, sliced and separated into rings
1 medium tomato, diced
1 can (4 oz.) OLD EL PASO Chopped Green Chilies
3 tablespoons vegetable oil
2 tablespoons vinegar
1 tablespoon dried cilantro
   salt

In a glass or porcelain bowl, cover the fish with lime or lemon juice. Marinate for more than 4 hours or overnight in the refrigerator. Turn once or twice to be sure that all surfaces are "cooked" by the citrus juice. Turn the fish into a colander; drain. Rinse lightly with cold water but not enough to wash out the juice. Return fish to bowl. Add onion, tomato, green chilies, oil, vinegar, cilantro and salt to taste. Mix gently. Serve chilled. Makes 4 to 6 servings.

Marinade gives fish a "pickled" flavor. Ideal light, warm weather luncheon dish.

MARINATED FILLET OLÉ

1 pound halibut or cod

¼ cup lemon juice

½ cup flour

1 tablespoon paprika, divided usage

1 teaspoon salt, divided usage

¼ cup salad oil

¾ cup vinegar

1 small onion, sliced

1 bay leaf

1 can (4 oz.) OLD EL PASO Chopped Green Chilies

1 tablespoon sugar

1 teaspoon cumin

½ teaspoon oregano leaves, crushed

½ teaspoon ground nutmeg

⅛ teaspoon garlic powder

⅛ teaspoon red pepper

Cut fish into 5 to 6 portions. Place fish in a shallow dish in a single layer. Pour lemon juice over top; let stand 15 minutes. Combine flour, 1 teaspoon paprika and ½ teaspoon salt. Coat fish with flour mixture. In a large skillet, heat oil until hot. Add fish; saute until opaque on inside and lightly browned on the outside, about 1½ to 2 minutes on each side. Place fish close together in a dish in a single layer. In a small saucepan, combine vinegar, onion, bay leaf, green chilies, sugar, remaining ½ teaspoon salt, cumin, oregano, nutmeg, garlic powder and red pepper. Bring to a boil; simmer covered 5 minutes. Pour over fish. Cover and refrigerate overnight. Serve on a bed of lettuce. Garnish with lemon wedges, stuffed olives and radish roses, if desired. Makes 5 to 6 servings.

MAIN DISHES
Meat

SOFT TACOS

1½ pounds ground beef

2 packages OLD EL PASO Taco Seasoning Mix

1 cup water

1 can (10 oz.) OLD EL PASO Enchilada Sauce

1 can (10¾ oz.) cream of mushroom soup

1 can (10¾ oz.) tomato soup

18 OLD EL PASO Taco Shells

1 cup (4 oz.) shredded Cheddar cheese

Brown ground beef in skillet; drain fat. Add taco seasoning mix and water. Stir. Bring to a boil, reduce heat and simmer uncovered 15 to 20 minutes, stirring occasionally, until liquid is reduced. Preheat oven to 350°F. Combine enchilada sauce and soups. Set aside. Spoon meat mixture into taco shells. Arrange shells in two 9x9-inch squared pans, in upright position, by leaning them against each other. Pour combined sauces over the shells evenly. Sprinkle with cheese. Bake for 15 minutes. Makes 18 tacos.

A delicious casserole with interesting flavor and texture contrast.

TACO CHIP CASSEROLE

1 pound ground beef
1 cup halved zucchini slices
½ cup chopped onion
1 jar (8 oz.) OLD EL PASO Mild Taco Sauce
1 can (16 oz.) tomato paste
1 jar (8 oz.) pasteurized process cheese spread
1 box (7½ oz.) OLD EL PASO NACHIPS Tortilla Chips

Brown ground beef in large skillet. Drain fat. Add zucchini and onion and cook until tender. Stir in taco sauce and tomato paste. Preheat oven to 375°F. In a 1½-quart baking dish, layer half of the meat mixture and process cheese spread; top with NACHIPS, repeat. Bake for 20 minutes. Garnish with additional NACHIPS, if desired. Makes 6 servings.

ENCHILADA CASSEROLE

1 pound ground beef
½ cup chopped green onions
1 can (14 oz.) OLD EL PASO Hot Enchilada Sauce, divided usage
1 teaspoon salt
12 OLD EL PASO Corn Tortillas
1 can (16 oz.) OLD EL PASO Refried Beans or OLD EL PASO Refried Beans with Green Chilies or OLD EL PASO Refried Beans with Sausage
2 cups (8 oz.) shredded Longhorn Cheddar cheese
½ cup sliced black olives

Brown ground beef and onion in medium skillet. Drain fat. Stir in ½ can enchilada sauce and salt; simmer for 5 minutes. Dip tortillas, one at a time, in hot oil for a few seconds on each side until limp. Drain on paper towels. Preheat oven to 375°F. Combine remaining enchilada sauce with beans. Spread ½ cup on bottom of 13 x 9-inch baking dish. Arrange 3 tortillas in a layer, top with ⅓ of bean mixture, ⅓ of meat mixture and ¼ of cheese. Repeat two more times. Tear remaining tortillas into small pieces. Arrange on top. Sprinkle with remaining ¼ cheese and top with olives. Bake for 20 minutes, until hot and bubbly. Makes 6 to 8 servings.

MICROCOOK on full power 10 to 12 minutes or until heated through. Turn once during cooking time.

MEXICAN LASAGNA

1 pound ground beef

½ cup chopped onion

1 envelope (1¼ oz.) OLD EL PASO Taco Seasoning Mix

1 can (8 oz.) tomato sauce

1 can (15 oz.) OLD EL PASO Mexe-Beans

1 can (4 oz.) OLD EL PASO Chopped Green Chilies

6 flour tortillas, 8-inch, halved, divided usage

2 cups (8 oz.) shredded Cheddar cheese, divided usage

Brown ground beef and onion in large skillet. Drain fat. Stir in seasoning mix, tomato sauce, mexe-beans and green chilies. Preheat oven to 350°F. Layer half of tortillas on bottom of 12 x 8-inch baking dish. Spread half of meat mixture over, and sprinkle with half of cheese. Repeat layers. Bake for 30 minutes. Let stand 10 minutes before serving. Makes 6 to 8 servings.

MICROCOOK on full power 16 to 18 minutes or until heated through. Turn 3 to 4 times during cooking time.

BEEF BIRDS

2 pounds beef round or sirloin steak, cut into 5 or 6 portions

½ cup chopped dill pickle

1 can (4 oz.) OLD EL PASO Chopped Green Chilies

2 tablespoons chopped green onions

3 slices bacon, fried, drained and crumbled

1 cup beef broth

salt and pepper

Preheat oven to 325°F. Flatten steak portions with a meat mallet. Combine pickle, green chilies, onion and bacon. Place 2 to 3 tablespoons pickle mixture on each piece of steak. Roll meat jelly roll fashion. Secure with toothpicks. Brown in 1-inch of hot fat; drain. Place in an 8-inch square baking dish. Repeat with remaining beef birds. Pour beef broth over, cover and bake for 1 hour, or until meat is tender. Salt and pepper to taste. Makes 5 to 6 beef birds.

A nutritious main dish or snack.

TOSTADA PIZZA

1¼ cups flour

1 teaspoon baking powder

½ teaspoon salt

½ cup milk

2 tablespoons vegetable oil

1 pound ground beef

1 envelope (1¼ oz.) OLD EL PASO Taco Seasoning Mix

1 can (16 oz.) OLD EL PASO Refried Beans or OLD EL PASO Refried Beans with Green Chilies or OLD EL PASO Refried Beans with Sausage

1 cup (4 oz.) shredded sharp American cheese

1 jar (8 oz.) OLD EL PASO Taco Sauce

1 can (4 oz.) OLD EL PASO Chopped Green Chilies

½ cup chopped onion

½ cup chopped tomatoes

1 cup shredded lettuce

Preheat oven to 425°F. Combine flour, baking powder, salt, milk and oil in bowl. Stir until mixture cleans sides of bowl. Press into a ball. Knead in bowl 10 times. Roll on lightly floured board to a 13-inch circle. Place on pizza pan or baking sheet. Turn up edge and pinch. Bake for 5 minutes. Prepare ground beef according to directions on seasoning mix package. Spread beans over crust. Top with meat mixture. Bake for 10 minutes, or until crust is lightly browned. Sprinkle cheese over. Bake 2 minutes longer. Top the pizza with taco sauce, green chilies, onion, tomato and shredded lettuce. Makes 8 servings, or one 13-inch pizza.

Preceding page: Tostada Pizza

BEEF SPINACH ROULADE

1 egg

1 pound ground beef

1 medium onion, chopped

1 can (4 oz.) OLD EL PASO Chopped Green Chilies

½ cup OLD EL PASO Taco Sauce

1 teaspoon salt

1 cup fresh bread crumbs

⅓ cup milk

⅓ cup PET Instant Nonfat Dry Milk

1 package (10 oz.) frozen chopped spinach, thawed

½ cup chopped celery

2 long slices Mozzarella cheese, cut into 4 triangles

OLD EL PASO Taco Sauce

Beat egg until blended in a large bowl; add ground beef, onion, green chilies, taco sauce, salt, bread crumbs, milk and instant nonfat dry milk; mix lightly until well blended. Pat mixture into a 12 x 9-inch rectangle on a sheet of waxed paper. Preheat oven to 350°F. Squeeze as much liquid as possible from spinach; place spinach evenly over meat; sprinkle celery on top. Using waxed paper as a guide, start at short end, roll meat jelly roll fashion; pinch ends and edges to seal. Place roll, seam-side down in a shallow baking dish. Bake 55 minutes or until loaf is firm and browned. Arrange triangles of cheese over loaf. Bake 5 minutes longer or until cheese melts. Place loaf on a serving platter, cut crosswise into thick slices. Serve with taco sauce. Makes 6 servings.

An impressive dish, spicy but not hot, ideal for company.

STUFFED FLANK STEAK

1½ pounds flank steak

¼ cup vinegar

1 teaspoon salt

½ teaspoon pepper

2 eggs

1 can (4 oz.) OLD EL PASO Whole Green Chilies, cut
    in strips

2 tablespoons chopped pimiento

2 tablespoons vegetable oil

1 tablespoon chopped onion

1 small clove garlic, minced

2 tablespoons flour

1 teaspoon chili powder

2 cups beef broth

  chopped parsley

Open the steak by splitting it to form two "pages," leaving a
hinge so that you have a single extended steak that covers twice
the area of the original. This cut should be made in such a
direction that the cutting edge of the knife is moving parallel to
the grain of the meat. Season the meat with the vinegar, salt and
pepper. Beat eggs and cook in a small skillet until set. Cut into
strips. Arrange the strips of egg and chilies, alternately over the
extended meat, parallel to the grain. Sprinkle with chopped
pimiento. Roll the meat so the grain runs the length of the roll
and tie securely in several places with string. Heat oil, fry the
rolled meat on all sides until brown; reserve drippings. Place in
baking pan. Preheat oven to 350°F. Add the onion and garlic to
the drippings in the frying pan, and cook a few minutes. Add
flour and chili powder; cook 2 minutes. Add broth and mix well.
Cook over low heat for 5 minutes to thicken. Pour sauce over the
rolled meat and bake; basting occasionally for 1 hour for medium
rare, or 1½ hours for well done. top with chopped parsley.
Makes 4 to 6 servings.

Dinner (Overleaf):   Seviche, Chicken and Vermicelli Soup, Stuffed
Flank Steak (served with taco sauce), Green Rice, Café Ice Cream.

These are traditional enchiladas with the tortillas fried, filled and rolled, then baked with Enchilada Sauce. For a more piquant flavor use "hot" Enchilada Sauce.

BEEF AND BEAN ENCHILADAS

1 pound ground beef

½ cup chopped onion

1 package (1¼ oz.) OLD EL PASO Taco Seasoning Mix

1 can (16 oz.) OLD EL PASO Refried Beans or OLD EL PASO
        Refried Beans with Green Chilies or OLD EL PASO
        Refried Beans with Sausage

1 can (10½ oz.) beef consomme, divided usage

1 can (11 oz.) OLD EL PASO Corn Tortillas

1 can (10 oz.) OLD EL PASO Enchilada Sauce

1 large tomato, chopped

1 cup (4 oz.) shredded Cheddar cheese

Brown ground beef and onion in large skillet. Drain fat. Stir in seasoning mix, beans and ½ cup consomme. Cook over medium heat until thickened, stirring occasionally, about 10 to 15 minutes. Remove from heat. Fry tortillas, one at a time in hot oil for a few seconds on each side, until limp. Drain on paper towels. Preheat oven to 375°F. Fill each tortilla with ¼ cup meat mixture. Roll tightly and place seam-side down in a 13x9-inch baking dish. Combine remaining consomme with enchilada sauce. Pour over enchiladas. Sprinkle with tomato and cheese. Bake for 15 to 20 minutes. Cool slightly. Makes 6 to 8 servings.

MICROCOOK uncovered on full power 10 to 12 minutes or until heated through. Turn once during cooking time.

BURRITO BEEF BAKE

    1 pound ground beef
½ cup chopped onion
    1 package (1¼ oz.) OLD EL PASO Taco Seasoning Mix
    1 can (10½ oz.) beef broth
    1 cup sliced fresh mushrooms
    1 small can (5.33 fl. oz.) PET Evaporated Milk
    2 cups (8 oz.) shredded process American cheese
12 flour tortillas, 10-inch
    OLD EL PASO Taco Sauce

Brown ground beef and onion in medium skillet. Drain fat. Stir in seasoning mix and broth. Simmer 20 minutes. Stir in mushrooms. Reserve a few for garnish. Set aside. Preheat oven to 350°F. In a small heavy saucepan combine evaporated milk and cheese. Cook over low heat until cheese is melted. Place ¼ cup meat mixture near one end of each tortilla. Fold nearest edge over to cover meat. Fold in both sides envelope fashion. Roll and place seam-side down in a 13x9-inch baking dish. Pour cheese sauce over and sprinkle with remaining mushroom slices. Bake for 15 to 20 minutes or until heated through. Serve immediately with taco sauce. Makes 5 servings.

MICROCOOK uncovered on full power for 10 to 12 minutes or until heated through. Turn once during cooking time.

A hearty meal-in-one with Mexican flavors.

GREEN CHILI STEW

2 pounds boneless pork butt
2 tablespoons vegetable oil
1 onion, chopped
1 large clove garlic, minced
2 teaspoons flour
1 can (15 oz.) OLD EL PASO Mexe-Beans
1 jar (8 oz.) OLD EL PASO Taco Sauce
2 cans (4 oz. each) OLD EL PASO Chopped Green Chilies
1 can (10 oz.) OLD EL PASO Tomatoes and Green Chilies
   salt and pepper

Trim off fat and cut pork into 1-inch cubes. Heat oil in a large heavy pot or Dutch oven. Add pork and cook until browned. Add onion and garlic. Cook until tender. Stir in flour. Cook and stir 1 to 2 minutes. Add mexe-beans, taco sauce, green chilies and tomatoes and green chilies. Season with salt and pepper to taste. Cover and simmer over low heat 1½ hours or until meat is tender. Makes 4 servings.

Following page: Green Chili Stew

MEXICAN HASH

1 pound ground pork
2 pounds ground beef or veal
1 chopped onion
1 jar (16 oz.) OLD EL PASO Taco Sauce
¼ cup chopped blanched almonds
¼ cup raisins (soaked in a small amount of water)
1 container (4 oz.) candied citron, chopped
2 small bananas, sliced (optional)
½ cup diced black olives
1 can (4 oz.) OLD EL PASO Chopped Green Chilies
1 tablespoon chopped parsley
1 stick cinnamon
2 cloves
   dash of cumin powder
1 tablespoon sugar
   salt and pepper

Brown ground meat and onion in large skillet. Drain fat. Add taco sauce and mix well. Add the almonds, raisins, citron, banana slices, olives, green chilies and parsley. Season with cinnamon, cloves, cumin, sugar, salt and pepper. Bring to a boil. Reduce to a simmer and cook for 30 to 35 minutes, or until mixture is thick. Stir occasionally to prevent sticking. Remove cinnamon stick and cloves before serving. Makes 10 to 12 servings.

This sauce freezes well.

SOUTH OF THE BORDER SPAGHETTI SAUCE

1 pound ground beef
1 medium onion, chopped
1 can (2 oz.) mushroom stems and pieces
1 can (10 oz.) OLD EL PASO Tomatoes and Green Chilies
1 can (8 oz.) tomato sauce
1 can (10 oz.) OLD EL PASO Enchilada Sauce
½ teaspoon salt
1 package (8 oz.) spaghetti, cooked and drained

Brown ground beef and onion in large skillet. Drain fat. Add mushrooms, tomatoes and green chilies, tomato sauce, enchilada sauce and salt. Simmer uncovered for 30 minutes, stirring occasionally. Serve hot over cooked spaghetti. Makes 4 to 6 servings.

A very nutritious meal, with selections from each of the four food groups.

FIESTA CHEESE BURGERS

1 egg

¼ cup OLD EL PASO Taco Sauce

¾ cup dry bread crumbs

1 can (4 oz.) OLD EL PASO Chopped Green Chilies

½ teaspoon salt

1½ pounds ground beef

8 slices (8 oz.) American cheese

8 hamburger buns

In a bowl combine egg, taco sauce, bread crumbs, green chilies and salt. Add ground beef ; mix thoroughly. Shape into 8 patties. Grill over medium coals for 8 to 10 minutes. Turn and grill until desired doneness. Add 1 slice of cheese to each patty and cook until melted. Serve on buns. Makes 8 servings.

For the palate more accustomed to hotter Southwestern flavors.

PICANTE STEAK STRIPS

1¾ pounds round steak

3 tablespoons vegetable oil

1 medium green pepper, diced

1 small onion, chopped

1 can (4 oz.) OLD EL PASO Chopped Green Chilies

1 large clove garlic, minced

1 can (8¼ oz.) stewed tomatoes, drained

1 can (10 oz.) OLD EL PASO Tomatoes and Green Chilies

1 teaspoon Worcestershire sauce

1 teaspoon dried oregano, crushed

salt and pepper

Cut meat in 1½ x ¼-inch strips. Heat oil in a large heavy skillet over high heat. Add meat strips. Cook until browned. Reduce heat. Add green pepper, onion, green chilies and garlic. Cook until vegetables are limp. Add stewed tomatoes, tomatoes and green chilies, Worcestershire sauce, oregano, salt and pepper to taste. Cover and simmer 1 hour or until meat is tender. Makes 6 servings.

PORK-CHILI ROLL UPS

3 pounds pork, cut in 1-inch cubes

2 tablespoons oil

2 small onions, chopped

2 cloves garlic, minced

2 medium green peppers, cut in strips

1 can (7 oz.) OLD EL PASO Chopped Green Chilies

1 teaspoon oregano

½ teaspoon ground cumin

1½ teaspoons salt

2 tablespoons cilantro leaves

1 tablespoon wine vinegar

¼ cup white wine

flour tortillas, warmed

shredded cheese

sour cream

guacamole (see recipe page 19)

Fry meat in oil until light brown. Remove meat; saute onion, garlic and green peppers in remaining oil. Return meat to pan. Stir in chilies, oregano, cumin, salt and cilantro; add vinegar and wine. Cover, simmer until meat is tender, about 2 hours. Skim off fat. Serve in warm tortillas with shredded cheese, sour cream and guacamole. Roll and serve. Makes 4 to 6 servings.

Preceding page: Mexi-Brunch Eggs

MAIN DISHES
Poultry

CHICKEN ELOQUENTE

2-2½ pounds frying chicken, cut up and seasoned
1 tablespoon olive oil
1 medium onion, finely chopped
1 clove garlic, minced
½ cup diced, cooked ham
1 cup dry white wine
1 can (4 oz.) OLD EL PASO Chopped Green Chilies
½ pound peeled, deveined, medium shrimp
¼ teaspoon paprika
1 tablespoon minced parsley
1 tablespoon corn starch
¼ cup cold water

Dust seasoned chicen pieces lightly with flour. Heat oil in deep skillet; brown chicken on all sides. Remove chicken from pan; add onion, garlic and ham to remaining oil. Stir. When tender, add wine, chilies, shrimp, paprika and parsley. Replace chicken; cover; simmer 45 minutes. Remove chicken and place on heated platter; keep warm. Add corn starch to cold water; stir into sauce and cook until thickened. Spoon sauce over chicken; garnish with parsley. Serve over hot rice. Make 4 servings.

SAUCY CHICKEN QUESADILLAS

2 cans (4 oz. each) OLD EL PASO Chopped Green Chilies
1½ cups (6 oz.) shredded Cheddar cheese
1 cup shredded, cooked chicken
8 flour tortillas, 8-inch
1 can (10 oz.) OLD EL PASO Hot Enchilada Sauce
1 can (10¾ oz.) cream of mushroom soup
1 can (10¾ oz.) tomato soup

Slit chilies; remove seeds and ribs. Cut chilies into strips lengthwise. Place an equal number of chili strips near one end of each tortilla. Combine 1 cup each, cheese and chicken. Sprinkle each tortilla with approximately ¼ cup of cheese mixture over chilies. Roll up securely. Place seam-side down in a 13x9-inch baking dish. Combine enchilada sauce and soups. Pour mixture over tortillas and top with remaining Cheddar cheese (approximately ½ cup). Bake at 350°F for 10 to 15 minutes or until bubbly. Makes 8 Enchiladas.

CHICKEN IN RED SESAME SAUCE

¼ cup toasted sesame seeds

¼ teaspoon cayenne pepper

6 chicken legs with thighs attached (3 lbs.)

4 tablespoons lard

1 large onion, finely chopped

2 cloves garlic, minced

2 cans (10 oz. each) OLD EL PASO Chopped Tomatoes
      and Green Chilies

1 tablespoon corn starch

1 can (4 oz.) OLD EL PASO Chopped Green Chilies

1 tablespoon chili powder

1 teaspoon salt

½ teaspoon ground cinnamon

½ teaspoon coriander

¼ teaspoon ground cloves

¼ teaspoon crushed anise seeds

   salt and pepper

   hot cooked rice, optional

Combine sesame seeds and pepper. Brown chicken legs on all sides in heated lard in a large frying pan. Spoon off fat. Add onion, garlic, tomatoes and green chilies, corn starch, green chilies, chili powder, salt, cinnamon, coriander, cloves, anise seeds and sesame seed mixture. Bring to a boil; cover, reduce heat and simmer for 1 hour or until chicken is tender. Remove chicken. Bring sauce to a boil and cook stirring frequently, until sauce is reduced and thickened. Salt and pepper to taste. Serve with rice, if desired. Makes 6 servings.

To toast sesame seeds: Spread in a shallow pan; bake in preheated 350°F oven stirring occasionally for 5 to 7 minutes or until golden brown.

Preceding page: Chicken in Red Sesame Sauce with Avocado Salad

Good recipe for leftover or canned chicken.

CHICKEN TACOS

½ cup chopped onion

2 tablespoons butter

2 cups shredded, cooked chicken

1 jar (8 oz.) OLD EL PASO Taco Sauce

1 envelope (1¼ oz.) OLD EL PASO Taco Seasoning Mix

12 OLD EL PASO Taco Shells

    shredded lettuce

    diced tomatoes

    sliced avocado

    sour cream

    OLD EL PASO Taco Sauce

Saute onion in butter in medium skillet until translucent. Stir in chicken, taco sauce and seasoning mix. Simmer, uncovered, over low heat for 15 minutes. Meanwhile, heat taco shells according to package directions. Spoon chicken mixture into taco shells. Top with lettuce, tomatoes, avocado and a dollop of sour cream. Serve with taco sauce. Makes 12 tacos.

A meal-in-one skillet dish.

YUCATAN CHICKEN

6 strips bacon, halved

¼ cup vegetable oil

1 frying chicken, sectioned and seasoned

1 small onion, chopped

1 clove garlic, minced

1 cup rice

1 can (10 oz.) OLD EL PASO Tomatoes and Green Chilies

1 can (4 oz.) OLD EL PASO Chopped Green Chilies

¼ teaspoon cumin

1½ cups chicken broth

1 cup frozen peas, cooked

Fry bacon in a large skillet; remove from pan. Add oil to the bacon fat. Fry the chicken for 10 to 15 minutes. Set aside. Saute onion, garlic and rice in the same pan for 3 minutes. Drain well in colander. Return to skillet. Stir in the tomatoes and green chilies, green chilies and cumin. Add the chicken and bacon. Pour chicken broth over mixture and cover tightly; simmer for 30 minutes. Stir in peas and serve. Makes 4 to 6 servings.

ACAPULCO CHICKEN

6 chicken breasts, skins removed

6 tablespoons butter, divided usage

2 cups chicken broth

½ cup chopped celery

½ cup PET Evaporated Milk, heated

1 tablespoon chopped parsley

¼ teaspoon salt
   dash of paprika

½ pound sliced mushrooms

1 can (10 oz.) OLD EL PASO Tomatoes and Green Chilies

1 onion, chopped

4 flour tortillas, 6-inch, cut in strips

3 cups (12 oz.) shredded Cheddar cheese
   OLD EL PASO Taco Sauce

Preheat oven to 450°F. Place chicken breasts in baking dish. Dot with 3 tablespoons butter. Cover with aluminum foil and bake for 45 minutes. Simmer chicken broth and celery until celery is tender. Spoon off fat. Add evaporated milk, chopped parsley, salt and paprika. Saute mushrooms in remaining 3 tablespoons butter and add to chicken broth. Add tomatoes and green chilies and onion. Heat sauce to just below boiling. Do not boil. Cover bottom of greased 13 x 9-inch baking dish with strips of flour tortillas. Pour ½ of broth over tortillas to moisten. Layer ½ of the chicken over the tortillas. Sprinkle ½ of the cheese over this. Repeat. Bake 45 minutes at 375°F. Serve with taco sauce, if desired. Makes 6 servings.

Overleaf: Enchiladas Suiza with Gazpacho Salad
Fiesta Casserole

ENCHILADAS SUIZA

3 cups shredded, cooked chicken

1 can (4 oz.) OLD EL PASO Chopped Green Chilies

1 teaspoon salt

1 can (10 oz.) OLD EL PASO Green Chili Enchilada Sauce

1 small can (5.33 fl. oz.) PET Evaporated Milk

12 OLD EL PASO Corn Tortillas

2 cups (8 oz.) shredded Monterey Jack cheese

Preheat oven to 425°F. Mix together chicken, green chilies and salt. Combine enchilada sauce and evaporated milk. Fry tortillas in a small amount of hot oil for a few seconds on each side until limp. Drain on paper towels. Dip each tortilla in enchilada sauce mixture; fill with ¼ cup chicken mixture; roll and place seam-side down in a 13 x 9-inch baking dish. Pour remaining sauce over. Sprinkle with cheese. Bake for 15 minutes or until bubbly. Makes 12 enchiladas.

MICROCOOK uncovered on full power for 8 to 12 minutes or until heated through. Turn once during cooking time.

Make-ahead casserole, flavorful but not zesty. Canned chicken makes it even easier.

FIESTA CASSEROLE

1 can (10¾ oz.) cream of chicken soup

1 jar (8 oz.) pasteurized process cheese spread

2 cups chopped, cooked or canned chicken

1 can (4 oz.) OLD EL PASO Chopped Green Chilies, drained

12 OLD EL PASO Corn Tortillas

1 can (10 oz.) OLD EL PASO Mild Enchilada Sauce

1-2 cups shredded lettuce

½ cup chopped tomatoes.

Preheat oven to 350°F. Combine soup and process cheese spread, mixing until well blended. Add chicken and green chilies. Spread ½ cup of chicken mixture over bottom of a 2-quart rectangular baking dish. Layer four of the tortillas, dipping each in enchilada sauce, and one third of the remaining chicken mixture; repeat layers two more times. Cover with foil; bake 20 minutes. Remove foil, continue baking 15 minutes. Top with lettuce and tomatoes. Makes 6 servings.

MICROCOOK uncovered on 70% power for 24 to 27 minutes or until heated through. Turn twice during cooking time.

CHICKEN CHILIES RELLENOS

3 boneless chicken breasts, halved

1 can (7 oz.) OLD EL PASO Whole Green Chilies

8 ounces Monterey Jack cheese or Cheddar cheese
(cut into 6 strips, 3 x ½ x ½-inch)

2 cups all-purpose flour

2 teaspoons salt

1 teaspoon pepper

½ teaspoon paprika

2 eggs

½ cup milk

OLD EL PASO Taco Sauce

Flatten chicken breasts with meat mallet. Slit chilies, removing
seeds and ribs. Place a chili on each chicken breast. Place a
piece of cheese on one end of a chili and roll the chicken breast
jelly roll fashion. Secure with toothpicks. Season flour with salt,
pepper and paprika. Beat together eggs and milk. Dip each
chicken roll in egg then flour. Repeat. Deep fry at 400°F for 10
minutes until golden brown. Drain on paper towels. Serve with
taco sauce. Makes 6 chicken chilies rellenos.

CHICKEN ENCHILADA CASSEROLE

12 OLD EL PASO Corn Tortillas

1 chicken, cooked, boned and diced

½ cup sliced black olives

1 can (4 oz.) OLD EL PASO Chopped Green Chilies

4 green onions, chopped

1½ cups (6 oz.) shredded Cheddar cheese

2 cups chicken broth

1 can (10½ oz.) cream of mushroom soup

1 can (10½ oz.) cream of chicken soup

salt and pepper

Preheat oven to 350°F. Cut tortillas into quarters. In a greased
13 x 9-inch baking dish, arrange a layer of tortillas and a layer
of chicken, olives, green chilies, onions and cheese. Repeat
layer. Mix chicken broth, mushroom and chicken soups and pour
over mixture. Top with more shredded cheese. Bake for 45 minutes.
Salt and pepper to taste. Makes 6 servings.

MICROCOOK uncovered on full power for 18 to 20 minutes or until
heated through. Turn twice during cooking time.

MAIN DISHES (POULTRY)

SALADS

TACO SALAD

1 pound ground beef
1 envelope (1¼ oz.) OLD EL PASO Taco Seasoning Mix
1 small head lettuce, torn in bite-size pieces (3 to 4 cups)
½ cup sliced black olives
1 cup (4 oz.) shredded sharp Cheddar cheese
1 large tomato, cut in wedges
1 small onion, thinly sliced and separated in rings
1 can (15 oz.) OLD EL PASO Garbanzo Beans, drained
   avocado slices
   coarsely crushed OLD EL PASO Taco or Tostada Shells
      or NACHIPS
   OLD EL PASO Taco Sauce

Prepare ground beef according to directions on seasoning mix package. In a salad bowl, combine lettuce, olives and cheese; toss well. Top with meat mixture, tomatoes, onion, garbanzo beans, avocado slices and broken taco shells. Serve with taco sauce. Makes 4 to 6 servings.

GAZPACHO SALAD

4 medium tomatoes, chopped
1 jar (8 oz.) OLD EL PASO Taco Sauce
2 tablespoons sherry wine or red wine vinegar
2 tablespoons chopped red onions
2 tablespoons chopped green onion
2 tablespoons OLD EL PASO Chopped Green Chilies
2 cloves garlic, finely minced
1 cup cucumber, chopped into ¼-inch cubes
¼ teaspoon coriander
2 tablespoons chopped basil leaves
¼ cup olive oil
   salt and pepper
   OLD EL PASO NACHIP Tortilla Chips

Combine all the ingredients in a mixing bowl, except the NACHIPS. Quantities of various ingredients may be increased according to taste. Chill. Serve with NACHIPS. Makes 4 to 6 servings.

AVOCADO SALAD

½ cup peeled and diced cucumber

2 green onions with tops, chopped

1 tablespoon chopped fresh parsley

1 cup OLD EL PASO Garbanzo Beans, drained

1 medium avocado, peeled, seeded and sliced

1 cup OLD EL PASO Taco Sauce

2 teaspoons olive oil

1 teaspoon cider vinegar

1 teaspoon lime juice

   lettuce leaves

Combine cucumber, green onions, parsley and garbanzos in a medium bowl; chill. Just before serving add avocado to cucumber mixture. Combine taco sauce, olive oil, vinegar and lime juice in a small bowl. Pour over avocado-cucumber mixture. Mix well. Spoon onto lettuce leaves. Makes 4 servings.

Easy make-ahead salad, particularly good for picnics.

FOUR-BEAN SALAD

1 can (15 oz.) OLD EL PASO Pinto Beans, drained

1 can (15 oz.) OLD EL PASO Garbanzo Beans, drained

1 can (8 oz.) cut green beans, drained

1 cup canned wax beans, drained

½ cup thinly sliced green pepper

¼ cup thinly sliced red onion

6 tablespoons vegetable oil

3 tablespoons vinegar

½ teaspoon salt

¼ teaspoon dried oregano

⅛ teaspoon garlic powder

   pepper to taste

1 tomato, chopped

3 tablespoons mayonnaise

Combine pinto beans, garbanzos, green beans and wax beans in a large bowl. Add green pepper and red onion. In a small jar mix oil, vinegar, salt, oregano, garlic powder and pepper to taste. Pour over salad and toss gently but thoroughly. Cover and refrigerate overnight. Just before serving, add tomatoes and mayonnaise. Toss until blended. Makes 6 to 8 servings.

SOUPS

WEST TEXAS CHILI

1 pound ground beef
1 can (15 oz.) OLD EL PASO Mexe-Beans
2 cans (10 oz. each) OLD EL PASO Tomatoes and
      Green Chilies
½ cup hot water
1 package (1⅜ oz.) OLD EL PASO Chili Seasoning Mix

Brown ground beef in skillet. Drain fat. Add mexe-beans, tomatoes and green chilies, hot water and chili seasoning mix. Bring to a boil, reduce heat and simmer uncovered for about 10 to 15 minutes. Makes about 5 cups.

Crisp Corn Tortillas in richly seasoned broth are nice flavor and texture combination.

TORTILLA SOUP

2 or 3 OLD EL PASO Corn Tortillas

    oil for frying

  2 teaspoons vegetable oil

  ⅓ cup chopped onion

  1 can (4 oz.) OLD EL PASO Chopped Green Chilies

  4 cups chicken broth

  1 cup shredded, cooked chicken

    salt

  1 can (10 oz.) OLD EL PASO Tomatoes and Green Chilies

  1 tablespoon lime juice

  4 large lime slices

Cut tortillas in 2 x ½-inch strips. Fry tortillas in small amount of hot oil until brown and crisp. Drain on paper towels. Heat 2 teaspoons of vegetable oil in a large saucepan. Add onion and saute until translucent. Add green chilies, broth, chicken, salt to taste, and tomatoes and green chilies. Cover and simmer 20 minutes. Stir in lime juice. To serve, pour into soup bowls and add tortilla strips. Float a lime slice in the center of each bowl. Makes 4 servings.

Preceding page: Tortilla Soup

TOMATO CHILI CHEESE SOUP

2 tablespoons vegetable oil
1 onion, finely chopped
4 green onions, finely chopped
1 clove garlic, minced
1 can (10 oz.) OLD EL PASO Tomatoes and Green Chilies
1 can (4 oz.) OLD EL PASO Chopped Green Chilies
1 tablespoon cilantro
2 cups water, divided usage
½ teaspoon salt
¼ teaspoon pepper
1 tall can (13 fl. oz.) PET Evaporated Milk
2 cups (8 oz.) shredded Monterey Jack cheese
1 cup (4 oz.) shredded American cheese
½ cup butter

Heat oil in a large saucepan. Add onion, green onions and garlic.
Cook until translucent. Add tomatoes and green chilies, green
chilies, cilantro, 1 cup water, salt and pepper. Simmer about
15 minutes. In another large saucepan, combine remaining 1 cup
water, evaporated milk, cheeses and butter. Stir over medium heat
until cheeses and butter are melted. Add tomato mixture. Stir
and simmer over medium heat about 10 minutes. Caution: Do
not let this mixture boil, it may curdle. Makes 8 servings.

A broth-type soup with a zesty flavor.

CHICKEN AND VERMICELLI SOUP

1 large chicken breast

6 cups water

1 small onion, sliced, divided usage

1 clove garlic

1 teaspoon salt

4 peppercorns

1 small onion, thinly sliced

1 can (10 oz.) OLD EL PASO Tomatoes and Green Chilies

2 cans (4 oz. each) OLD EL PASO Chopped Green Chilies

1 tablespoon cilantro

1 ounce vermicelli

Place chicken breast in a large saucepan. Add water, ½ onion, garlic, salt and peppercorns. Bring to a boil; reduce heat. Cover and simmer 45 minutes. Remove chicken and let cool slightly. Shred chicken meat, discarding skin and bones. Strain broth; return chicken to broth. Add remaining onion to soup. Bring to a boil. Add tomatoes and green chilies, green chilies, cilantro and vermicelli. Cook 15 minutes. Taste and add salt if needed. Makes 6 servings.

Make ahead to serve cold; but when serving hot, heat and serve immediately. When reheated, avocados turn brown.

AVOCADO CREAM SOUP

1½-2 large ripe avocados, peeled and seeded
   ½ teaspoon garlic salt
   1 cup PET Evaporated Milk
   2 teaspoons lemon juice
   ½ cup OLD EL PASO Taco Sauce
   2 tablespoons OLD EL PASO Chopped Green Chilies
   2 cups chicken broth

Place avocados, garlic salt, evaporated milk, lemon juice, taco sauce and green chilies in blender. Blend well. Heat chicken broth. Remove from heat and cool slightly. Add puree to warm broth. Stir well. Serve hot or cold. Garnish with a dallop of sour cream and a thin slice of lime, avocado or sprig of cilantro. Makes 6 servings.

CREAM OF ZUCCHINI SOUP

4 medium zucchini
2 cups water
   salt
2 tablespoons chopped fresh parsley
2 cans (4 oz. each) OLD EL PASO Chopped Green Chilies
2 tablespoons butter
2 tablespoons finely chopped onion
1 tablespoon flour
1 tall can (13 fl. oz.) PET Evaporated Milk
1 cup chicken broth
   parsley leaves for garnish

Wash zucchini. Cut off stem ends, then cut in large pieces. Place in a large saucepan. Add water and a pinch of salt. Bring to a boil. Cover and cook until tender, about 20 minutes. Remove zucchini, let cool. Place zucchini, 1 cup cooking liquid, parsley and green chilies in blender, blend until pureed. Heat butter in medium saucepan; add onion. Cook until translucent. Stir in flour. Cook and stir one minute. Add pureed zucchini mixture, evaporated milk and chicken broth. Stir to blend. Season with salt if needed. Stir over medium heat for 10 to 15 minutes, just below boiling. Serve at once or chill and serve cold. Garnish with a few parsley leaves. Makes 6 servings.

Following page: Avocado Cream Soup

GREEN CHILI SOUP

3 green peppers
1 can (4 oz.) OLD EL PASO Chopped Green Chilies
1 small onion, chopped
½ cup PET Evaporated Milk
4 beef bouillon cubes
4 cups boiling water
2 tablespoons butter
2 tablespoons flour
1 cup diced ham
2 medium carrots, shredded
½ teaspoon salt
¼ teaspoon pepper
2 packages (3 oz. each) cream cheese

Cut tops off green peppers, remove seeds and ribs and discard. Simmer in water in a covered saucepan for 20 minutes or until tender. Section the green peppers and combine with green chilies, onion and evaporated milk and blend until smooth; set aside. Drop bouillon cubes into boiling water. Let boil until dissolved. Melt butter in a large saucepan and blend in flour. Stirring constantly, gradually add the green pepper mixture, bouillon, diced ham, carrots, salt and pepper. Stir until soup is thickened and smooth. Serve hot with generous dabs of cream cheese. Makes 6 servings.

Delicious version of this classic cold soup.

GAZPACHO SOUP

5 slices bread, crusts removed

1½ cups water

1 cucumber, cut in large chunks

1 green pepper, cut in large chunks

1 onion, cut in large chunks

2 cloves garlic, cut up

1 quart tomatoes

2 cans (4 oz. each) OLD EL PASO Chopped Green Chilies

¼ cup red wine vinegar

¼ cup olive oil

1 teaspoon salt

Cut bread slices into quarters; soften in water. Place about 1/3 of the remaining ingredients and bread mixture in blender container and blend until smooth. Repeat with remaining ingredients until all is blended. Chill before serving. Makes 8 servings.

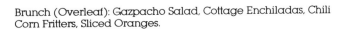

Brunch (Overleaf): Gazpacho Salad, Cottage Enchiladas, Chili Corn Fritters, Sliced Oranges.

VEGETABLES

CHILI COLESLAW

1 medium cabbage, shredded

1 can (4 oz.) OLD EL PASO Chopped Green Chilies

1 medium onion, sliced

2 tablespoons lemon juice

2 teaspoons salt

1 teaspoon celery seed

¼ cup vinegar

⅓ cup water

¼ cup olive oil

⅓ cup sugar

Combine cabbage, green chilies and onion. Pour lemon juice over and toss. Season with the salt and celery seed. Make a dressing with the vinegar, water, olive oil and sugar. Pour over salad and refrigerate for at least 1 hour before serving. Makes 6 servings.

MEXICAN STUFFED ZUCCHINI

3 medium zucchini

1 can (10 oz.) OLD EL PASO Enchilada Sauce

½ cup water

1 slice bacon, chopped

¼ cup chopped green pepper

1 can (4 oz.) OLD EL PASO Chopped Green Chilies

1 small onion, chopped

1 cup chopped mushrooms

1 clove garlic, minced

½ cup canned corn

¼ cup sliced black olives

1½ cups cooked rice

1 cup OLD EL PASO Taco Sauce

1 egg, beaten

¼ teaspoon salt

⅛ teaspoon pepper

½ cup grated dry Parmesan cheese

Preheat oven to 325°F. Slice the zucchini in half lengthwise and scoop out and discard seeds and pulp. Combine enchilada sauce and water in a large shallow baking dish. Then place the zucchini in the dish skin-side down and steam in oven under foil for 30 minutes, or until tender. Meanwhile, saute bacon; drain. Add green pepper, green chilies, onion, mushrooms. and garlic. Cook until onion is translucent. Remove from heat and add corn, olives, rice, taco sauce, egg, salt and pepper. Mix together. Scoop mixture into zucchini shells and top with cheese. Cover again with foil and bake until zucchini is tender, approximately 35 minutes. Makes 6 servings.

Easy and impressive to make at the table.

CARROTS FLAMED WITH TEQUILA

5 medium carrots, (1 lb.)
  boiling salted water
3 tablespoons butter
¼ cup OLD EL PASO Chopped Green Chilies
¼ teaspoon dried dill weed, crushed
¼ teaspoon salt
⅛ teaspoon pepper
¼ cup tequila, warmed

Peel carrots, cut in thin diagonal slices. Cook in boiling salted water 10 minutes; drain. Melt butter in skillet or serving dish. Add carrots. Saute 2 to 3 minutes. Add green chilies, dill weed, salt and pepper. Add warm tequila; ignite. When flames go down, stir and serve. Makes 4 servings.

Corn dishes are traditional in Mexican cooking.

GREEN CORN CASSEROLE

1 can (4 oz.) OLD EL PASO Whole Green Chilies
3 cups corn, cooked and drained
⅓ cup yellow corn meal
2 tablespoons butter, melted
2 teaspoons sugar
½-1 teaspoon salt
1 cup (4 oz.) shredded Cheddar cheese
1 can (10 oz.) OLD EL PASO Tomatoes and Green Chilies
½ teaspoon dried oregano

Preheat oven to 350°F. Butter a 1-quart baking dish; set aside. Rinse chilies and cut into long strips. Combine corn, corn meal, butter, sugar and salt in medium mixing bowl. Mix well. Layer half the corn mixture in buttered baking dish. Top evenly with all the chili strips. Sprinkle with cheese. Top with remaining corn mixture. Cover with foil; bake 1 hour. Heat tomatoes and green chilies and oregano in a small saucepan. Serve as a sauce with the casserole. Makes 6 servings.

Preceding page: Carrots Flamed with Tequila

DESSERTS

CREAMY PECAN PIE

1 package (3¼ oz.) vanilla pudding and pie filling
1 cup dark corn syrup
¾ cup PET Evaporated Milk
1 egg, slightly beaten
1 cup chopped pecans
1 frozen PET-RITZ Regular Pie Crust Shell

Preheat oven to 375°F. Blend together pudding mix and corn syrup. Gradually stir in evaporated milk and egg. Add pecans. Pour into pie shell. Bake until top is firm and just begins to crack, about 40 minutes. Cool at least 3 hours before serving. Makes one 9-inch pie.

CAFÉ ICE CREAM

2 eggs
½ cup sugar
4 cups PET Evaporated Milk
1-2 tablespoons instant coffee
½ cup coffee liqueur

Beat eggs and sugar in large mixing bowl until well blended. Scald evaporated milk and coffee over medium heat until bubbles appear along edge. Gradually stir about 2 cups of the hot evaporated milk mixture into the egg mixture. Blend into remaining hot milk mixture. Cook and stir over low heat until mixture thickens slightly. Remove from heat. Refrigerate until well chilled. Stir in coffee liqueur. Pour into ice cream freezer container. Churn and freeze according to manufacturer's directions. Makes 2 quarts.

Preceding page: Chimichangas

RUM FLAN

1¼ cups sugar, divided usage

  4 eggs

  2 cups PET Evaporated Milk

  2 cups milk

  2 tablespoons dark rum or 1 tablespoon rum flavoring

  ¼ teaspoon salt

Preheat oven to 350°F. In skillet place ½ cup sugar over low heat, watching carefully, allow sugar to melt and turn brown (caramelize). Pour caramelized sugar into flan pan, or 2-quart casserole, or souffle dish. Rotate until bottom is covered. Beat eggs and remaining ¾ cup sugar in large mixing bowl. Add evaporated milk, milk, rum and salt. Mix well. Pour milk mixture into mold. Place the mold in a large pan. Pour warm water into the larger pan halfway up the sides of the mold. Bake about 1 hour and 45 minutes to 2 hours, or until knife inserted halfway into flan comes out clean (do not pierce bottom). Chill for several hours. Unmold. Makes 6-8 servings.

Candy is a nice way to end a meal.

ALMOND TOFFEE CANDY

1 cup slivered almonds

1 stick (½ cup) butter

1 cup sugar

½ teaspoon salt

¼ cup water

4 ounces milk chocolate

Place almonds on a well-greased baking sheet. Set aside. Combine butter, sugar, salt and water in small saucepan and cook over medium heat for 20 minutes or until mixture turns a light brown color. Pour this over the almonds and let cool. Melt chocolate in a double boiler. Spread the chocolate evenly over the toffee mixture. Freeze until firm.

MICROCOOK butter, sugar, salt and water on full power for 8 to 12 minutes. MICROCOOK chocolate on 50% power for 2 minutes.

COFFEE LIQUEUR PIE

1 PET-RITZ Regular Pie Crust Shell, baked

1 small can (5.33 fl. oz.) PET Evaporated Milk

½ cup semi-sweet chocolate pieces

2 cups miniature marshmallows

⅓ cup chopped almonds, toasted

⅓ cup coffee liqueur

1 container (12 oz.) PET WHIP Non-Dairy Whipped
      Topping, thawed

  Maraschino cherries

Combine evaporated milk and chocolate pieces in heavy
1-quart saucepan. Cook over low heat, stirring occasionally,
until chocolate melts completely and mixture thickens. Stir in
marshmallows until melted. Remove from heat. Add almonds.
Pour into a 2-quart bowl and refrigerate until cool (about 20 to
30 minutes), stirring twice. Add coffee liqueur. Fold in whipped
topping. Spoon into baked pie shell. Freeze several hours until
firm. Remove from freezer 10 minutes before serving for ease in
cutting. If desired, garnish with additional Pet Whip, chopped
almonds and maraschino cherries. Makes 8 servings.

To toast almonds: Place almonds on baking sheet in preheated
350°F oven, stirring frequently until almonds are lightly toasted,
about 10 minutes.

Puffy Sopaipillas are traditionally served with honey but are also
good sprinkled with cinnamon and sugar.

SOPAIPILLAS

  4 cups all-purpose flour, sifted

  2 tablespoons baking powder

  1 teaspoon salt

  3 tablespoons shortening

1-1½ cups water

    honey

Sift together flour, baking powder and salt. Cut in shortening.
Add enough water to make a soft dough. Roll out dough until it is
¼-inch thick. Cut into 3-inch squares and deep fry at 400°F until
golden brown. Drain on paper towels. Serve warm with honey.

Following page: Sopaipillas and Coffee Liqueur Pie

An easy, light dessert. Bananas are wrapped in flour tortillas, seasoned with spices and served hot with a choice of orange or chocolate sauce or both.

TOASTED BANANAS

6 large firm, ripe bananas

3 tablespoons lemon juice

12 flour tortillas

⅔ cup sugar

1 teaspoon cinnamon

⅛ teaspoon nutmeg

¼ cup milk

Preheat oven to 400°F. Peel bananas and cut in half lengthwise; dip in lemon juice. Place each slice at one end of a tortilla. Stir together sugar, cinnamon and nutmeg; sprinkle over bananas. Reserve a small amount for top. Roll each tortilla and secure with a toothpick. Brush tortilla lightly with milk and sprinkle with remaining cinnamon-sugar mixture. Place on a well-greased baking sheet and bake at 400°F for 15 minutes. Remove from baking sheet immediately. Serve with orange sauce or chocolate sauce. Makes 12 servings.

Orange Sauce:

¼ cup sugar

1 tablespoon corn starch

1 cup orange juice

1 tablespoon butter

1 tablespoon lemon juice

Chocolate Sauce:

1 (8 oz.) milk chocolate bar

1 small can (5.33 fl. oz.) PET Evaporated Milk

pinch of salt

1 teaspoon vanilla

Orange Sauce: Mix together sugar and corn starch; add orange juice and cook, stirring until thickened. Stir in butter and lemon juice. Serve warm with bananas.

Chocolate Sauce: Melt chocolate in a double boiler. Add evaporated milk and salt. Cook until slightly thickened, about 10 minutes; stirring constantly. Stir in vanilla. Serve warm with bananas.

RECIPE INDEX

RECIPE INDEX

OLD EL PASO